The Complete

OPEN

OBEDIENCE COURSE

by

BLANCHE SAUNDERS

Illustrated by Gloria Strang

Copyright © 1969 by Howell Book House Inc.
© 1961, Blanche Saunders
Library of Congress Catalog Card Number: 61-14206
Printed in U.S.A.   ISBN 0-87605-751-2

Fifth Printing—1971

HOWELL BOOK HOUSE INC.

845 Third Avenue, New York, N. Y. 10022

TABLE OF CONTENTS

THE DOG IN TRAINING

The dog in training should be in good physical condition and should receive the necessary inoculations to safeguard her* health. Before each training session:

Feed lightly

Exercise thoroughly

Give a small amount of water

Groom for comfort and appearances' sake

Having attended to your dog's needs, be serious, but not domineering, about the training. When making corrections, it is not so much WHAT you do as the WAY in which you do it.

---

* Editor's Note: Throughout this book the dog is referred to as *her*, in the interest of simplicity. This does not mean that male dogs are poor performers or any more difficult to train than females.

OPEN CLASS EQUIPMENT

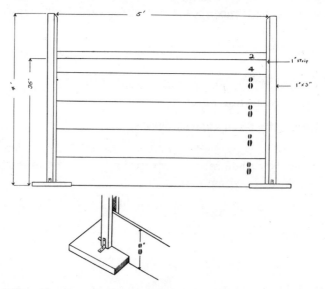

The Solid Hurdle. Detailed specifications may be found in The American and Canadian Kennel Club rule books for Obedience Trials.

The High Jump: Five feet wide. Adjustable in heights of from eight to thirty-six inches. Consists of four 1" x 8" boards, one 1" x 4" board and two 4-foot Standard uprights, each with a wide base, constructed with grooves into which the boards fit. (See **Regulations and Standards for Obedience Trials,** available from: The American Kennel Club, 51 Madison Ave., New York, N.Y. 10010 and The Canadian Kennel Club, 667 Yonge Street, Toronto, Canada.)

Note: One 1" x 2" board may be necessary to meet certain height requirements.

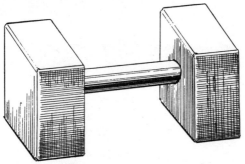

Paint it a light color.

The Dumbbell: Available in small, medium, and large sizes. Select a dumbbell made of hardwood and with square ends. End pieces should be sufficiently large to discourage the dog from picking the dumbbell up the wrong way.

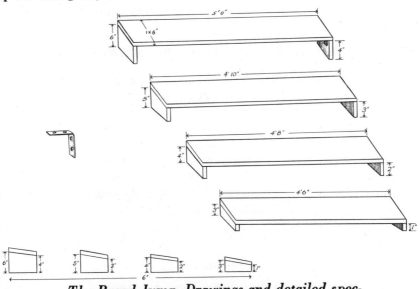

The Broad Jump. Drawings and detailed specifications may be found in the rule books.

The Broad Jump: Consists of two to four separate hurdles, five feet long and 8 inches wide, measuring 1 inch to 6 inches in height and adjustable from 16 inches to 72 inches in overall length. The flat surface of each hurdle slopes, allowing for a 2 inch difference in height between the front and the back edge of each hurdle. The hurdles are constructed in such a way that they telescope for convenient storage. **(See Regulations and Standards for Obedience Trials.)**

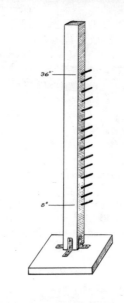

*The Bar Hurdle. This is not part of the Open
Course but is used for the jumping exercises.*

The Bar Jump: The Bar Jump is not part of the OPEN CLASS
equipment, but it will be used in the JUMPING exercise. Construction
is similar to that of the High Jump. Instead of boards, a square 2 to
2½″ wooden horizontal bar is used, which is adjustable for raising or
lowering according to the height of the dog. Adjustable for each 2
inches of height from 8 inches to 36 inches. (See **Regulations and
Standards for Obedience Trials.**)

Miscellaneous Training Equipment:

Training collar and a six-foot flat leather leash.

A long line with a snap on one end.

A small, rolled magazine.

A light rod, approximately 4 feet long (for clearing the High
Jump.)

A piece of chicken wire or hardware cloth, the size of the Broad
Jump.

TRAINING SUGGESTIONS

Plan your dog's schooling so training for the OPEN CLASS will be a series of progressive lessons. Long, long before you start the OPEN work, condition your dog for advanced training by encouraging her, while she is young (yes, even as a puppy), to carry assorted articles, to retrieve thrown objects and to leap small hurdles. If your older dog is just starting her Obedience career, include carrying and jumping as part of her Novice work. Owners can pave the way for the OPEN and UTILITY Classes without affecting a dog's performance while still competing in the Novice Class.

Timing is important! When you teach voice commands, give the command. Follow with the correction and praise.

When you teach hand signals, give the signal. Follow with the correction and praise.

When you want your dog to heel or to come, use her name with the command.

When you want the dog to perform at a distance, stress the command or give a signal without the name.

Give a command or signal ONCE. Repeat when necessary but put a correction with it.

Praise AFTER commands and signals and WITH corrections. The praise must be discontinued when exhibiting in Obedience Trials, but when used during the training period, your dog will be more responsive.

When you praise, BE SINCERE! Dogs respond to a cajoling tone of voice.

Modify your method of training to the SIZE AND TEMPERAMENT of the dog. Not all dogs train alike!

When you correct, disguise corrections so you and your assistant will not appear responsible.

If you inadvertently make a harsh correction or misjudge the timing, make up to your dog immediately; then be careful not to repeat the mistake.

If you find that one of the suggested corrective methods has a bad effect on **your** dog, don't use it. Dogs react differently to corrections.

When problems come up, work backward. If your dog won't retrieve over the hurdle, lower the jump until she gains confidence. If she won't **retrieve on flat**, go back to the HOLDING and "TAKE IT!" exercises. Praise and a fresh start have a magical effect when a dog is temporarily confused.

If you use your hand at any time to reprimand your dog (such as cuffing the dog's nose for creeping), pat her with the SAME hand you used to correct her. Your dog must think the hand correction was accidental.

Don't be surprised when you attempt to solve one problem if your dog slips back on some other part of the exercise. For instance, if you have been correcting your dog for NOT coming, she will undoubtedly come a few times TOO soon. The setback, while discouraging, is temporary, and in time you will balance the training.

A good trainer will never use food as the ONLY inducement for making a dog obedient, but if your slow performer peps up when you give food, use it to overcome problems.

If you are NOT successful in your training, BE MORE DEMANDING. Each time you correct for a REPEATED mistake, use a firmer tone of voice and jerk the leash harder.

Strive for perfection from the beginning. When you are careless about little things, they become problems later on.

The suggestions offered in **The Complete Open Obedience Course** will be more effective if your dog received the basic training outlined in **The Complete Novice Obedience Course.**

The instructions given in the succeeding sections of this book are for people who are right-handed. Those who are left-handed may follow the same instructions, simply substituting the left hand for the right, and the right hand for the left. However, in Obedience Trials a dog must heel on the handler's left side.

For the purpose of teaching, the OPEN class exercises are broken down to include:

Heeling

Drop In The Distance

Drop On Recall

Retrieve In Play

Holding On Command

Carrying On Command

Jumping

Jumping While Carrying

The "Take it!"

Reaching For The Dumbbell While Walking

Picking Up The Dumbbell From The Ground

Picking Up The Dumbbell On Command While Walking

Retrieve On Flat

Retrieve Over Hurdle

The Broad Jump

SIT- AND DOWN-STAYS (Handlers out of sight)

What may prove to be a difficult situation with one dog during training for the advanced work, will present no problem for another. By dividing the OPEN CLASS work into **exercises,** rather than weekly lessons, owners can select that part of the text instruction that applies to the needs of their dog.

HEELING

Heeling With Turns

Perfection in FREE HEELING is achieved through leash training. Study your dog's natural movements and select a speed suitable to the dog. The heeling exercises will then be a normal procedure, based on the dog's physical and mental characteristics. If you have not already done so, get into the habit of starting the heeling action with your LEFT foot. In the Novice work, it didn't matter which foot you started on, because the Novice exhibitor normally uses the heeling command. Then too, when working with a large untrained dog, the trainer has better balance when he starts on the right foot. For the advanced training, teach your dog that when your RIGHT foot moves, it means to STAY. When your LEFT foot steps forward, it means to FOLLOW.

A common mistake made by amateur trainers is to jerk the leash when they step forward at the start of the heeling exercise. This TIMING is incorrect! There should be no hand movement, only the verbal command, such as "Robin, Heel!" which is given before the foot moves. The leash is jerked AFTER the trainer starts, while the foot is coming down on the first step, and WHILE the trainer is giving praise. A gentle patting of the side follows EVERY jerk of the leash.

The majority of dogs perform with accuracy when the leash is on but will take advantage on the HEEL FREE. To overcome this independent attitude, surprise your dog by USING the leash when she doesn't expect it. During the heeling routine, turn sharply at short intervals and catch her off guard. AFTER you turn, tug on the leash forcefully, using a minimum of hand motion but with exaggerated praise. Do this two or three times, then make the turns WITHOUT jerking the leash but GIVE PRAISE JUST THE SAME. If the leash is used continuously, your dog will heel wider than ever, or will heel close through fear.

Practice about-turns from a standstill. As you pivot, reach back with your RIGHT foot and tap the dog lightly on the right flank. Bring your feet together, reach down and pat her immediately. The dog must think the foot correction was unintentional. But you accomplished your purpose by making her turn.

Make one complete circle to the right, first while in motion, and again from a stand. Circling keeps a dog alert and watchful of movements. If it is a big dog you are training, reach back with your right hand when you make an about-turn, and "spank" the dog playfully on the rear. When she looks around in surprise, clap your hands in front of your body and coax her to come close at heel. Encouraging your dog to remain at heel position through cleverly disguised tricks is a better method of training than jerking the collar repeatedly.

Fast And Slow

During the heeling exercise, dash forward and snap the leash **with praise.** Slow to a walk, and say a quiet "Good Girl!" Do a fast run **without** jerking the leash, but give praise just the same. The praise can be dropped after your dog has learned to change pace, but during the teaching stage, the dog will be more responsive if she thinks the jerk on the leash is part of a running game.

The Figure 8

Train your dog to do a close Figure 8 the same way you taught her to do the Fast and the Slow. Circle two posts, two chairs, or two of anything, placed approximately six feet apart. When your dog is on the outside of the circle, SPEED UP, jerk the leash with a series of snaps and give praise. When the dog is on the inside of the circle, slow to a walk, while you continue the praise. The third or fourth time you circle the "posts" with the dog on the outside, speed up without jerking the leash, and when the dog changes pace, praise her for doing so.

Bring your feet together BEFORE you correct for sitting ahead.

Sits

Wad the leash into a ball and hold it in your LEFT hand. Keep your elbow straight with your arm close to your body. Go through the heeling routine and make the necessary heeling corrections in a playful manner. When you halt, bring your feet together, WAIT, and see what happens. If your dog passes your knee, snap the leash backward with force to make her sit immediately. Give praise when you do it. If the dog stops when you stop, but continues to stand, or is slow to sit, transfer the leash to your right hand and, with the left, "spank" her to a sitting position, then follow with exaggerated patting with the SAME hand. Even a small dog will accept corrections cheerfully, working happily and with spirit, when corrections are made the right way.

Finishes

With the leash in your LEFT hand and your dog at heel position, hold your arm close to your side with elbow STRAIGHT. Command "Heel!" and take one step to the RIGHT. Give praise and jerk the leash IN BACK of your body to make the dog move with you.

Make a quarter turn to the LEFT. Pivot on your left foot, don't step! Say "Heel!" and snap the leash backward to make your dog square herself around to sit at the proper heel position. Don't forget the praise!

A series of BACKWARD steps will help teach your dog the correct heel position. Step back with your LEFT foot, command "Heel!" and snap the leash backward, again with praise. Before you realize it, your dog will automatically shift her position whenever you move away from her or when you turn your body.

Say "Stay!" and with the leash still in your LEFT hand, face your dog. Stand directly in front of her. Hold your left elbow STRAIGHT! Tell her "Robin, Heel!" then WAIT, for you must do one of three things: If the dog starts on command, praise her as she moves around to your left side, but don't move your arm. If she doesn't start on command, snap the leash past your side and give praise simultaneously. If she moves around to your side on command but does a sloppy finish, wait until she starts to sit, THEN jerk further back to make her do a more complete finish. Give praise when you use the leash.

If you have trained your dog to go to heel position by going to the RIGHT and around in back, make corrections with the RIGHT hand.

Practice the heeling exercises with the leash thrown loosely over your shoulder or tucked under your belt, and with your hands at your waist or at your side. Correct each mistake by snapping the leash sharply, then let go of it at once. Follow each correction with a gentle patting of your left side to encourage the dog.

FREE HEELING

When you take the leash off, remember the following:

Walk in a straight line. Angling into your dog will cause her to heel wide.

Walk briskly! Don't adapt your pace to that of the dog.

Hold your LEFT hand close to your body!

Give the first command in a happy tone of voice.

Change to a demanding tone or call your dog's name sharply if she lags or ambles away. AFTER the second command, gently pat your side and give praise.

If forging is your problem, or if your dog attempts to dart away, STAND STILL! Signal back with your left hand and repeat the heel command forcefully, then pat your side coaxingly.

When your dog is doing a good job of FREE HEELING, give her credit! Praise her while she is working. The praise can be discontinued AFTER THE DOG IS TRAINED, but while learning, every dog needs encouragement.

If you are training a large dog, carry the leash folded twice, with the snap end in your RIGHT hand. If the dog fails to pay attention, call her name loudly or reach out and "spank" her playfully on the hindquarters with the end of the leash, then coax her close by patting your side.

If all attempts to keep your dog at heel position fail, snap on the leash, give it ONE good jerk to bring the dog in close, and try again. The change in voice, followed by flattery, with the occasional use of the leash, should eventually teach your dog to stay at your side at all times. Especially if you make the heeling fun! On every halt, avoid stepping into your dog. The foot that is furthest back is brought forward to meet the foot in front. When the action is in reverse (toward the dog) the dog will draw away, fearful of being stepped on.

When teaching your dog FREE HEELING for the OPEN Course, the length of the practice sessions will vary, depending upon the dog. Short lessons with generous praise and patting, with the offering of a few tempting tid-bits, are generally effective. Far more important, by keeping the training a pleasant experience, you will have a HAPPY working dog!

HEELING Problems—How To Overcome Them

Forging

Leash corrections can be made by an assistant who walks at the dog's left, while holding the leash in the RIGHT hand. The owner commands "Heel!" When the dog forges, the assistant jerks backward on the leash while the owner gives praise.

For off-leash corrections, the assistant walks backward in front of the dog. After the owner gives the heel command, if the dog forges, the assistant tosses some object (an empty cardboard carton is excellent) directly in front of the dog, or bangs on the floor with a rolled magazine. These are excellent corrections for instructors to use with unruly dogs in a Beginner's Class. For proper timing, the owner must give the heel command before the instructor makes the correction.

Lagging And Heeling Wide

Lagging and wide heeling are difficult problems to overcome once they become a habit. There is no one magical cure. If your dog is the greedy type, carry food to encourage her to stay close. When you take the leash off, have a fishline or a strong piece of string already attached to the collar so you can make corrections when the dog doesn't expect them. If the dog is not the scary type, ask three or four assistants to help by dropping articles surreptitiously, and ONE AT A TIME; or to push some object, such as an empty carton or a folding chair, toward the dog when she lags or heels wide. Tapping the floor with a long pole in back of the dog is also effective. Be careful not to overdo corrections and be generous with praise.

Dog Lags On The Figure 8

Hold the leash in BOTH hands, low and close to your body. When the dog is on the INSIDE of the circle, walk naturally. When she is on the OUTSIDE, speed up, jerk the leash in a series of snaps, giving praise. About the third or fourth time around, speed up WITHOUT jerking the leash, but give praise just the same. This teaches your dog to change pace, an important feature of the

Figure 8. When you take the leash off, walk naturally but continue with the praise until your dog consistently remains close.

Dog Is Slow To Sit On The Halt

Put the dog on leash. Wad the leash into a ball and hold it in your LEFT hand. Keep your elbow straight. AFTER your feet come together, jerk the leash backward with force to make the dog sit. The important thing is not to be moving your feet at the time you jerk the leash.

### LARGE DOGS	### SMALL DOGS
An assistant at the dog's left can spank the dog to a sitting position AFTER the handler halts. Don't forget the praise.	Carry a light rod in your RIGHT hand. The leash in your LEFT. After you halt, reach in back of your body and tap the dog gently, but firmly, on the hindquarters.

Dog Heels On Wrong Side

Reach back with your RIGHT hand and cuff the dog's nose when she comes in on your right side. After which, pat your left leg with your LEFT hand to encourage her to heel there.

Carry something in your RIGHT hand, firm but soft, that just clears the floor. Make the same correction. Or, kick back with your RIGHT foot when the dog comes in on the right.

Heavy-Set Dog Fails To Change Pace

Heel the dog between two people. When you run, give praise. If the dog doesn't run with you, the person on the dog's left jerks the leash forward, with BOTH hands. When the leash is off, continue giving praise when you change pace, until the dog thinks running is part of the game.

16

HEELING Problems—How To Overcome Them

Dog Bites At Hand

Hold the LEFT hand still. Slap the dog's nose with the RIGHT hand. At the same time, tell her "Stop it!"

Dog Lags And Is Wide On The Right-About-Turn

LARGE DOGS

"Spank" your dog when you make the turn. Reach back with your RIGHT hand or your RIGHT foot and tap the dog's hindquarters, then clap your hands playfully in front of your body, to encourage her to come close.

SMALL DOGS

Put your dog back on leash and make sharper corrections.

Dog Nips Ankle On The Fast

Ask an assistant to hold a small, rolled magazine or the leash wadded into a ball. When your dog barks or nips your ankle when you run, have the assistant throw what she is holding at the dog's feet and tell the dog "Stop that!" Give praise, especially when your dog will run without misbehaving.

Dog Sits Ahead

LARGE DOGS

The correction is the same as for slow sits. After you halt, jerk backward on the leash, held in the LEFT hand.

Or, have an assistant make the correction from the dog's left.

SMALL DOGS

Same, but in a more gentle manner, although the severity of the correction really depends upon the temperament of the dog.

Alternate correction: Bring the leash in back of your body and hold it in your RIGHT hand. After you halt, jerk the leash to the right. Give praise!

17

Playful corrections get excellent results.

Dog Sits At An Angle

Walk the dog between two people. If she swings her hindquarters AWAY from the handler, the person on the dog's left taps the dog on the hip to make her sit straight.

Same, but done gently with a light rod held in the RIGHT hand. Or, the assistant can use the heel of her right foot.

If the crooked sit is in the opposite direction, the handler reaches back with her RIGHT foot and taps the dog on the right hip to make her straighten the sit.

Dog Heels And Sits Wide

With the dog on leash, walk her close to a wall or a fence. If she goes wide and bumps into the barrier, she may correct herself, especially if you encourage her to stay close to your side. If she veers away when you halt, pull the leash tight WITHOUT JERKING IT, and hold her until she sits close.

Wide heeling is usually the result of jerking the leash without adequate praise. It also comes from grabbing for the dog while she is heeling free. Wide sits are the result of stepping into the dog on the halts.

DROP IN THE DISTANCE

Owners of Novice dogs would do well to postpone the DROP ON RECALL until their dogs have gained the C.D. degree. The "drop," which sometimes slows a dog up on the COME, could result in lower scores while the dog is competing in the Novice Classes. Practicing the DROP IN THE DISTANCE, however, alternating it with the COME, and the SIT and STAY, is good training experience for the dog.

Before you attempt to make your dog drop at a distance, teach her first to drop directly in front of you on the FIRST command and on the FIRST signal. With the dog on leash, facing you, hold the leash in your LEFT hand (it is presumed, of course, that your dog already knows how to lie down as outlined in **The Complete Novice Obedience Course**). WITHOUT MOVING YOUR BODY, command "Down!" Use a quiet tone of voice and follow the command with "Good Girl!" The praise is important! It encourages the dog to obey without leash correction. If one is necessary, it will be more favorably received. If your dog obeys the first command to lie down, go to YOUR right, circle around in back, and while she is in the down position, pat her. If the command is ignored, quickly stamp on the leash with your RIGHT foot to get her down, giving EXTRA praise. Circle around, pat her, but don't let her get up until you give her permission. With a small dog, or one that is extra sensitive, tap the leash more gently.

Certain dogs, especially Hounds and Toy breeds, resent the snap on the collar used to put a dog down. In this case, lean over so your hands are close to the dog. Give the command, and, if ignored, BUMP the palm of your hand ONCE against the dog's nose, PUSH her to a down position by pressing on her shoulders, then pat her or scratch her ear. The bump on the nose can be most effective when used the RIGHT way. The right way is with fingers pointing UP.

After your dog lies down on voice command, tell her "Sit!" This time raise your RIGHT hand (this is the signal used by right-handed people to make the dog lie down) and follow the signal with "Good Girl!" If your dog isn't down by the time your hand is raised with fingers pointing UP, stamp on the leash or bump the palm of the raised hand against the dog's nose, with EXTRA praise. Say "DOWN!" at the same time, then circle around to heel position and pat her while she is lying down. The important things to remember are these: Give the command WITHOUT BODY MOTION; when you use the signal, raise your hand, WAIT, then make the correction; and whether you use your hand or your foot to get your dog down, give PRAISE! The way you give the signal is also important. Lift your hand quickly, then lower it slowly while the dog is in the process of going down. If you drop the hand too fast, it will look like the signal to come and your dog could be confused.

When your dog will lie down immediately on a single command, and will do the same when you give the signal, try it without the leash, but stay close to your dog. Give the command or signal ONCE, then follow with praise. The praise can be dropped AFTER the dog has learned to react immediately, but during the teaching, praise should accompany the voice and the hand gesture. When the leash is off, and the command or signal is ignored, the bump on the nose is an effective correction. Return to heel position each time your dog goes down; pat her or give her a tasty morsel so she will associate something pleasant with the prone position.

Gradually increase the distance you stand away, but ONLY if your dog will drop immediately, on a single command or signal, a distance equal to the length of the leash. With the dog some distance away, the VOICE now becomes the correction. When the command or signal is ignored, give the second command **demandingly.**

The ultimate goal for the DROP IN THE DISTANCE should be twenty-five to thirty feet, to prepare your dog for DROP ON RECALL.

If you still have trouble making your dog lie down at a distance, fasten a long line to her collar and run the line through a ring in the floor, or one placed in the ground. Ask an assistant to hold the end of the line at a distance (or hold the line yourself). Tell your dog "Stay!" Face her, then give the signal or the command to lie down. If she remains sitting, the pull on the line will put her down. Return, make her sit, and repeat the exercise.

DROP ON RECALL

When your dog is ready for the DROP ON RECALL, put her back on leash and face her at its full length. Call her by name, command "Come!" then follow with "Down! Good Girl!" Don't let the dog get up too much speed before you drop her. Give the command without bending your body, and DON'T YELL! If the training for DROP IN THE DISTANCE has been adequate, you should have little trouble with the DROP ON RECALL exercise. However, if your dog continues toward you after you give the command (and you had better be prepared for this), run forward, bump her nose gently with the palm of your hand, using a backhand motion (like that used when playing tennis), making the correction with as little hand motion as possible. After the dog lies down, pat her.

Practice a series of "drops." Call your dog, run backward, and, without leaning forward, tell her "Down!" After she is down, call her, run backward, and drop her again. Do this first by command and then by signal, following each drop with praise. Try the exercise off leash. Keep your body upright. Use the same calm voice you used when the leash was on, and give the same type of signal. If you yell or make frantic motions, your dog may think she has done something wrong and will try to dart away.

The distance you stand from your dog is gradually increased. She should also be made to drop at various distances from the spot where she is called. If you make your dog lie down in the SAME spot each

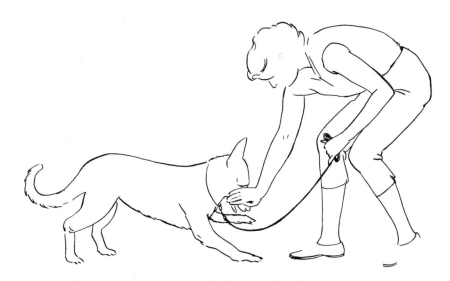

Used the RIGHT way, a bump on the nose stops creeping.

time, she will very likely anticipate the command and drop before she is told.

In practice, alternate the DROP ON RECALL with a straight RE-CALL and with the DROP IN THE DISTANCE. This will teach your dog to wait for commands, and not to act when she hears your voice. When training, give the command quietly. Signal the drop without too much violence.

DROP ON RECALL failures can usually be traced to yelling at the dog, thus frightening her, and to excessive body motion, which is confusing.

Things To Remember When Teaching DROP IN THE DISTANCE And The DROP ON RECALL

Keep the dog on leash.

Teach your dog to drop directly in front of you before you make her drop at a distance.

Without bending forward, tell your dog to drop (command or signal).

When you use a voice command, avoid yelling.

Train your dog to drop when you RAISE your hand.

If the dog doesn't obey the FIRST command or signal, bump her nose with the palm of your hand, or stamp on the leash forcefully. At the same time, say "DOWN!" and after the dog is down, pat her!

When you take the leash off, increase the distance you stand from the dog—but **not** if you have to tell her twice before she obeys.

When the command or signal is ignored at a distance, call out demandingly, "DOWN!" then **run** forward and make the necessary correction.

While the dog is learning, give praise WITH every command and WITH every signal.

After your dog knows the DROP ON RECALL, alternate with the straight RECALL, and with the DROP IN THE DISTANCE.

DROP ON RECALL Problems—How To Overcome Them

Dog Does Not Come On First Command

Ask someone to stand close to your dog. Get the dog's attention, then call her, and follow the command with praise. If she doesn't start, the assistant taps the dog on the rear with the toe of her shoe as though it were accidental. After she does it, clap your hands playfully, and give extra praise.

Tossing something at the dog from a hidden location will have the same effect; but take care that the dog does not see the object thrown or the person who threw it. Cover up every correction with play.

Dog Comes Before She Is Called

Leave your dog. Face her at the length of the training area. Hold something in your hand. If the dog starts before she is called, toss what you are holding in front to block her. Take her back and try again. In practice, alternate the come with the sit-stay.

Dog Is Slow To Drop On Command

With your dog on leash, face her at its full length. Call her and run BACKWARD. Before she catches up with you, and while you are still backing up, give a quiet command "Down!" then run FOR-WARD and bump the dog's nose gently with the palm of your hand. Use a backhand motion like that used when playing tennis, with fingers pointing UP. When the dog is down, praise and pat her.

Dog Is Slow To Drop On Signal

With your dog on leash, face her at its full length. Call her, run BACKWARD, and while still backing up, raise your hand, which is the signal to go down; then run FORWARD and bump the dog on the nose gently, with the palm of the SAME hand. Again, keep the fingers pointing UP! Pat the dog after she lies down.

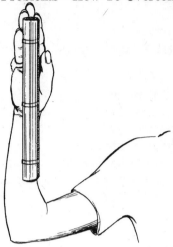

When you use corrective tools, disguise them.

Dog Continues Forward After Given Signal To Drop

Leave your dog, and face her at a distance. Hold a small, rolled magazine (taped in the center and on each end) along the palm and wrist of the hand you use to give the signal. Call your dog, signal the drop, and, if she obeys, say a quiet "Good Girl!" Complete the exercise the usual way. If she ignores the signal, toss the magazine directly in front of her, and while your hand is still raised, command "Down!" When she obeys, go to her, pat her, or give her something to eat as a reward.

Dog Comes Slowly When Called

After you call your dog, if she slows up, turn and RUN, or turn your back and clap your hands. Your dog should instinctively speed up. After she comes, if she likes to eat, give her food.

An assistant can toss a small object in back of the dog if the dog doesn't know he is there. Five things are important: (1) Do not let the dog see the object when it is thrown. (2) Give praise with the correction. (3) Throw the object only when necessary. (4) **After** the correction, run, clap your hands and make a game of the training. (5) Reward the dog when she comes, using food if necessary.

DROP ON RECALL Problems—How To Overcome Them

The line is effective with large dogs as well as small.

Dog Continues Forward After Commanded To Drop

Same as for not dropping on signal, EXCEPT that the magazine is tossed underhanded. Don't throw the magazine unless the dog ignores the command, and give praise with the correction. The leash rolled into a ball can be used the same way. The object is to check the dog's forward movement after the command has been ignored.

Alternate correction: Fasten the dog on a long line, equal in length to the distance the dog must travel BEFORE you drop her. Tie the other end of the line to a stationary object in back of the dog. Call her, then signal the down BEFORE she reaches the end of the line. When the line checks her, tell her "Down!" again, then go to her, and praise and pat her.

Note: When making a correction for DROP ON RECALL, there should be a pause between the giving of the command or signal and the throwing of an object. If the line is used to make the correction, the command or signal should be given BEFORE the dog reaches the end of the line. This is to give the dog a chance to obey before she is corrected for disobedience. Improper timing will cause a dog to fear the drop and look cowed.

27

DROP ON RECALL Problems—How To Overcome Them

Dog Anticipates Drop

Same as for coming slowly, but after the correction, call the dog straight without making her drop.

Dog Doesn't Come In A Straight Line And Veers To The Side On The Drop

Form a narrow aisle with two lines of people facing each other. As the dog passes down the center and is made to drop, ask your assistants to reassure the dog with quiet praise. Widen the aisle gradually.

Dog Stops On Signal But Remains Standing

Put your dog on leash, stand her, then ask an assistant to stand at the dog's side, with leash in hand. Tell your dog "Stay!" Face her some distance away, then give the command or signal to lie down. If the dog ignores it, the assistant makes the dog go down by pulling up on the leash, sliding it under her foot. Make the dog stand and repeat the lesson until she will lie down immediately on command or signal, from a standing position. With small dogs, the pull on the leash is gentle.

Alternate correction: Use the line through a ring in the floor or the ground, and practice pulling your dog down from a standing position.

Dog Anticipates Come After Drop

Call your dog. Drop her! After she drops, turn and walk away. If she starts to follow, DEMAND "STAY!" Return after a few moments, face her, and call her or go back to her and pat her while she is still lying down.

Practice calling another dog's name AFTER your dog has dropped. If your dog comes, call out "Down! Stay!" Let her learn to wait for HER name.

In practice, alternate the DROP ON RECALL with the DROP IN THE DISTANCE, and with the SIT-STAY exercises. This will teach your dog to wait for COMMANDS, not to act out a definite routine.

RETRIEVE IN PLAY

Teach your dog to carry while she is young.

As suggested earlier, holding, carrying, and retrieving do not have to be associated entirely with a dog's adult life, or with Obedience Trials. Even a young puppy can be taught to hold and carry if you place something in her mouth and encourage her with "Take it to so-and-so!" Carrying from one person to another thus becomes a game, and with it, comes a chance to show off. These early attempts at carrying will teach your dog, with a minimum of effort, the basic steps of the RETRIEVE exercise, one of the most difficult in advanced training.

If your dog is a natural retriever, take advantage! Make a game of retrieving objects, both in the house and out-of-doors. Concentrate on getting your dog excited so she will chase things, then just before she reaches the object, give the retrieve command ONCE. **While she is picking up the object**, say "Good Girl!" and say it as though you meant it. Praise will encourage a dog to take things from the floor or the ground when she might otherwise refuse.

If your dog starts for an object and comes back without it, or if she doesn't start at all, run to the object, pick it up, scuff it between her paws in a teasing manner, drag it along the floor, or kick it around; then place it in her mouth (unless she reaches for it herself), and turn and run. If she follows, clap your hands, squeal with delight, but DON'T REACH FOR WHAT SHE IS HOLDING. Let her strut around proudly, then, after a few moments, call her, quietly take the object away, and throw it again. If she won't give you the article when you say "Out!" cuff her gently on the nose with your free hand, and after she lets go, tell her "Good Girl!" and pat her.

Make your dog understand that after every retrieve she must bring the article back to you. For best results, kneel when you call her and give praise in a happy, high-pitched tone. If she starts running around with the article, change to a demanding "COME!" (throw your shoe or the leash at her if necessary) then coax her to come close by tapping the floor or the ground. When she comes, pat her before you take the article so she will learn to expect a pleasant reward for delivering things.

Train your dog to retrieve playfully while on leash. This will prepare her for leash corrections, which later may be necessary. While you hold the handle of the leash, make a game of throwing objects, letting the dog run after them. When she picks them up, don't forget the praise! If she sniffs the object, then walks away, kick it around like you would a football. Kick it first away from her, then toward her paws. Talk to her at the same time in a cajoling tone of voice to give encouragement. If she still won't pick it up, hand it to her, then try again.

RETRIEVE IN PLAY lessons should be short so your dog won't get tired of the game. You fail in your objective if the dog gets bored and refuses to pick up thrown articles in play. Another thing—don't always make your dog sit after she picks up the article. The steadying-down process required for Obedience Trials can be applied AFTER the dog has learned to retrieve on command. For the play training, keep things exciting.

When practicing RETRIEVE IN PLAY, use an assortment of articles for your games, and among them include the dumbbell. The retrieve exercise should not be associated with any one object. It is also important that you give the retrieve command just before your dog reaches for the article and that you praise enthusiastically while she is picking it up. Afterward, quietly but firmly insist that she bring the article to you.

Things To Remember When Teaching The RETRIEVE IN PLAY

Play games every chance you have.

Use an assortment of articles, and include the dumbbell.

Practice RETRIEVE IN PLAY, both on and off leash.

Keep the retrieve command a happy one.

Give the command ONCE.

Give praise while your dog is taking the article from the floor or the ground.

Allow your dog to chase articles without waiting for them to stop rolling.

Don't insist that the dog sit every time she returns.

When you take the object from your dog, never pull on it.

As the dog progresses, delay the praise until she is on her way back WITH the article.

Train often, but keep the lessons short.

If your dog has no interest in playing games, give her straight obedience. Owners with little previous experience can successfully teach their dogs to retrieve on command by following the instructions outlined on the following pages, but take ONE step at a time, and thoroughly master it before going on to the next!

HOLDING ON COMMAND

If you have taught your dog by playful means to **hold** what you give her, you can pass up this part of the training. The older dog that doesn't know what it means to carry things around will require the gentle, FIRM instructions outlined in this section.

The first lesson is to teach your dog to HOLD your finger. This isn't as dangerous as it sounds, because even a strange dog will seldom bite when handled in the proper manner. With your dog on leash and sitting at your left side, stretch the leash taut and step on it with your RIGHT foot. This will keep the dog from backing away. Gently place your LEFT hand around the dog's muzzle (unless it is a short-nosed breed, in which case, hold the skin on the side of the neck), and hook the little finger of your RIGHT hand under the collar beneath the dog's chin. By pulling the collar FORWARD, you apply pressure to the back of the neck, which keeps the dog from getting out of hand.

Place a finger or thumb very gently into the dog's mouth, holding it directly behind the canine teeth. When you do this, say "Take it! Good girl!" Press the jaws together, still giving praise, to keep the dog from mouthing your finger. When she holds without struggling, command "Out!" and take your finger away. Do this several times, then use an assortment of articles, including the dumbbell. MOVE SLOWLY! HANDLE QUIETLY! Don't forget the PRAISE!

The first HOLDING lesson. Holding your finger!

When you work with the dumbbell, keep your hands close to the dog.

Teach your dog to grip things securely! Take one end of the object and SHAKE it gently while it is in her mouth. If she tries to give it to you, tell her "Hold it! Hold it!" and don't permit her to let go until you command "OUT!"

Some dogs, no matter how calmly they are handled, become hysterical and fight desperately the first time an object is placed in their mouths. In this case, tighten your grip, momentarily, by pulling the collar FORWARD and UP. This brings pressure on the back of the dog's neck and lifts the front paws off the floor so the dog can't keep her balance. By clamping the jaws together and forcing her to hold what you give her, the struggle should cease immediately. Having won the battle, calmly lower the dog's feet to the floor, pat her, scratch her ear, then remove the object. (It is suggested that you use some object other than your finger for this part of the training.)

When your dog will hold an object without spitting it out, scratch her ear with one hand, but KEEP THE OTHER HAND UNDER THE DOG'S CHIN! If she lowers her head as though to drop the article, cuff her chin up, and tell her "Hold it! Hold it!" If she drops what she is holding, the correction is one sharp tug on the leash, a tap on the nose, and telling her "Phooey!" BEFORE you pick the article up from the floor to make her try again.

Practice the SIT-STAY exercise while your dog holds different articles, among them the dumbbell. Practice the RECALL while she carries them to you. After you call, TURN and walk away. This will teach your dog to carry while heeling, which she should do if you give the heeling command, or encourage her by saying enthusiastically, "Let's go!" When you halt, give a quiet "Sit-stay!" to keep the dumbbell in her mouth.

When teaching HOLDING ON COMMAND, avoid long training sessions. Five or ten minutes at a time is sufficiently long, and your dog won't get tired or become bored with the dumbbell work. Avoid training in extreme heat. Dogs perspire by panting. When the mouth must be open to breathe freely, the dog won't grip the object firmly.

Things To Remember When Teaching HOLDING ON COMMAND

Keep the dog on leash.

Flatter your dog while she is holding. Scratch her ear, stroke her head. This will take her mind off the desire to drop the article.

Hold your hands close to the dog while she is learning. Move quickly if you think she is going to drop what she is holding.

If the head goes down, tap your dog under the chin and say "Hold it! Hold it!"

Shake the article lightly while it is in the dog's mouth so she will learn to grip securely.

Keep lessons short.

Don't train when the weather is hot.

Don't train when the dog is panting from excitement.

Practice with articles made of wood, metal, leather and other material.

While your dog is holding, get her to a standing position by tickling her under the stomach.

Keep her standing by scratching her ear and giving praise.

If she decides to trot around, clap your hands, turn your back and walk away. Give extra praise.

When you pat your dog, keep your hands away from the head. Pat her on the rear instead.

Whenever she drops what she is holding, shame her, then correct with a tap on the nose or a tug on the collar, BEFORE you pick the article from the floor to try again.

Scratching the back makes holding easier.

When you take things from the dog, see that she lets go when you tell her. If she doesn't, cuff her nose ONCE with the free hand, or blow in her face. When she releases the article, praise her.

After your dog learns HOLDING ON COMMAND, hand her things whenever you have a chance. Insist upon obedience. Praise and pat her when she keeps things in her mouth. Correct her sharply when she drops things without permission. When she becomes dependable, she is ready for the next step, CARRYING ON COMMAND.

CARRYING ON COMMAND

If your dog will hold what you give her, either as the result of early puppy training or the methods described in HOLDING ON COMMAND, teach your dog to carry while on leash. Dogs often carry things by themselves but will drop what they are holding when the leash is on. Give your dog something to hold, then scratch her back or tickle her stomach to get her to a standing position. KEEP THE LEASH SLACK, and, if she has not yet dropped the article, turn your back, run, clap your hands (this has a magical effect), and say "Let's go!" Use a cajoling voice when you praise; and when you pat your dog, keep your hands away from the object she is carrying. Pat the hindquarters, not the head.

If your dog refuses to walk while holding, coax her! Tap the floor, and give praise in a high-pitched voice. If she decides she has nothing to fear, and will take a few steps toward you, stand up, TURN AND WALK AWAY. See if she will follow. The important thing is to keep the leash slack. The choking effect of a tight collar will cause a dog to drop what she is carrying.

A small dog will get accustomed to a forward motion while holding, if you pick her up and carry her a few steps. Gradually lower her to the floor, then stand behind her, and PUSH her gently from the rear. The habit of "freezing" when an article is placed in the mouth, can be overcome by quiet handling with generous praise.

Don't be surprised if your dog keeps dropping things you give her, and when she does, don't become impatient or annoyed. This is a crucial point in your dog's obedience career. It is better to take extra time to accomplish your objective than to make the dog dislike the carrying exercise because you are overly anxious.

Carry the small dog!

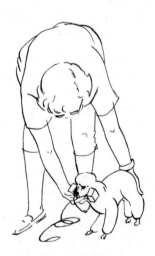

Push from the rear!

Things To Remember When Teaching CARRYING ON COMMAND

Train your dog, while she is young, to carry all sorts of articles.

When the dog is holding, and the leash is on, KEEP THE LEASH SLACK.

If your dog refuses to walk while carrying, coax her by tapping the floor, or push her gently from the rear. Scratch her back, tickle her stomach, but, most important of all, talk to her in "baby talk."

If your dog will hold the object, TURN AWAY, CLAP YOUR HANDS, and make a game of the carrying.

If she still hasn't dropped what she is holding, run with her in play.

Give praise in a high-pitched tone of voice. Dogs respond to cajolery.

If your dog keeps dropping the article through sheer stubbornness, be more firm with each correction without losing your temper or becoming impatient.

Praising and hand clapping work magic!

JUMPING

(The HUP!-HEEL Exercise)

Your dog may be a long way yet from retrieving, but why not brighten the training routine by teaching the JUMPING exercise? Place the Solid, the Bar, and the Broad Jumps in different parts of the training area. Keep the Hurdle and Bar Jumps LOW, and the Broad Jump NARROW. The jumps can be raised or widened after your dog has become an expert at leaping obstacles, but to simplify the training and make proper corrections, it is important that the jumping be ridiculously easy the first few times.

With your dog on leash, hold the leash in BOTH hands, as when teaching the heeling exercises. Approach the Bar and the Hurdle Jumps slowly, and STEP OVER with your dog. Keep the leash sufficiently taut so the dog can't dart off to one side. If she balks at the hurdle, **pull** her gently over, WITH PRAISE! If she ducks under the bar, cuff her nose to make her draw back, then encourage her to go over the top. When approaching the Broad Jump, speed up a little, and leap over WITH the dog.

The JUMPING command may be "Jump!" "Over!" or "Hup!" and should be given BEFORE the leash is used to pull the dog across. Avoid a lifting motion. Use a forward thrust that will not throw the dog off balance, and give praise while the dog is jumping. After she lands, command "Heel!" and jerk backward on the leash, PAT YOUR SIDE, and encourage the dog to walk at heel position. The important thing to keep in mind when teaching the JUMPING exercise is NEVER let your dog refuse a jump once you have given her the jumping command. Make her go over, even if you have to lower the jump almost to the floor, or tip the individual boards of the BROAD Jump on their sides. Refusing a jump, thus getting her way, will encourage her to balk whenever she feels like it.

When your dog is familiar with the different types of hurdles, and will leap them on command, it will no longer be necessary to step over with the dog. Walk past the hurdles instead, and meet her on the other side. While the dog is jumping, hold your LEFT arm away from your body so the leash extends STRAIGHT UP FROM THE CENTER OF THE HURDLE. While the dog is landing, drop your left arm, so as not to throw her off balance when she lands. After she jumps, slow down or come to a standstill, and command "Heel!" Snap backward on the leash, **pat your side,** and give praise.

When your dog will jump and stay at heel without corrections, try the JUMPING exercise without leash. Approach each hurdle in a fast walk, POINT TO IT WITH YOUR LEFT HAND, and give the jumping command. Pass by the hurdle quickly, slow down, command "Heel!" and signal backward and pat your side. Don't run when teaching JUMPING. Running gets a dog excited and causes confusion. As a result, you may inadvertently make a bad correction that could affect your dog's jumping career.

Whether schooling a dog for Obedience competition, or for fun and exercise, the accepted height of a jump for most breeds is one and one-half times the height your dog measures at the withers (this is from the top of the shoulder to the floor). Current Obedience Regulations provide the following exceptions:

> The jump shall be once the height of the dog at the withers, or 36 inches, whichever is less, for the following breeds: Bloodhounds, Bullmastiffs, Great Danes, Great Pyrenees, Mastiffs, Newfoundlands, St. Bernards. The jump shall be once the height of the dog at the withers, or 8 inches, whichever is greater, for the following breeds: Clumber Spaniels, Sussex Spaniels, Basset Hounds, Dachshunds, Cardigan Welsh Corgis, Pembroke Welsh Corgis, Australian Terriers, Cairn Terriers, Dandie Dinmont Terriers, Norwich Terriers, Scottish Terriers, Sealyham Terriers, Skye Terriers, West Highland White Terriers, Maltese, Pekingese, Bulldogs, French Bulldogs.

The Broad Jump is twice as wide as the height of the High Jump. For instance, if your dog measures 16 inches at the shoulder, she should jump 24 inches in height and 48 inches in length. Don't expect your dog to jump exaggerated distances. In her efforts to please, she could have a bad fall, or she may learn to climb the hurdle instead of clearing it, which, in Trials, counts as a penalty.

RECALL OVER THREE HURDLES

A cuff on the nose will teach your dog NOT to go under the bar.

As your dog progresses in the JUMPING exercise, set the three jumps in a row, approximately fifteen feet apart. This is a fun-exercise that is enjoyed by both dogs and owners. Place the Broad Jump on one side of the Solid Hurdle and the Bar Jump on the other. With your dog on leash, leave her on a sit-stay in front of a NARROW Broad Jump. Face her on the opposite side. Tell her "Jump!" then snap the leash toward you with praise. Tell her to sit, then pat her.

Lead her to the LOW Solid Hurdle. Tell her "Stay!" and face her from the opposite side. Stress the JUMPING command when you call her. After she jumps, make her sit, pat her, then move on to the Bar. The Bar Jump, too, must be absurdly LOW.

When your dog is reliable and will jump all three hurdles on leash, try them with the leash off. Use the command "Come!" and then encourage the dog to leap each hurdle by calling loudly "Jump!" "Hup!" or "Over!" Try one jump at a time until your dog knows this part of the exercise, then try two hurdles. Leave her in front of the Broad Jump while you go to the opposite side of the Solid Hurdle. Call her, and if she jumps the two, lead her to the Bar, and make her jump that. If she starts around the jumps at any time, run forward and block her, then coax her to come over the top.

After sufficient practice, try all three. Leave the dog sitting in front of the Broad Jump. Face her from the far side of the Bar Hurdle. Kneel, then call her. As she approaches each of the three hurdles, call out a loud jumping command, and follow each command with praise. The Bar Jump will be the most difficult of the three, unless you have taught your dog STICK JUMPING and she is familiar with a single bar. Stand close to the last jump, and be ready to block her from going around the end or from ducking under the bar. If she attempts either, cuff her nose gently with the back of your hand, then pat the top of the bar and encourage her to come over the top. With practice, your dog will soon learn to leap all three hurdles on command, a useful exercise for exhibition work.

Owners who have trouble with their dogs running around the hurdles in this exercise should ask six people to assist, one standing at each side of the three hurdles. If there are not enough assistants available, chairs or other objects can be used. The fact that someone is standing in the way or that some obstacle blocks each side of the jumps, will encourage the dog to leap over the top instead of running around the ends.

An alternate method is for an assistant to hold the dog's leash when she is left sitting in front of the Broad Jump. The owner, from in front of the Bar Jump, calls the dog while the assistant runs with the dog and guides her over each hurdle. Timing the command with the correction is important. The owner calls out the jumping command as the dog approaches each hurdle. The assistant tugs on the leash if the dog starts around the end.

Things To Remember When Teaching JUMPING

Teach your dog to jump obstacles of various shapes and sizes.

Keep the dog on leash until she knows how to jump.

Keep the jumps simple during the first few lessons.

During the "Hup! Heel!" exercise, leap the hurdles with your dog to give her confidence.

Give the jumping command BEFORE you use the leash to pull the dog across.

Move the leash over the jump AHEAD of the dog.

Give praise while the dog is jumping.

Never permit your dog to balk at a hurdle. If she does, pull her slowly across.

If your dog tries to duck under the bar, cuff her nose with the back of your hand to make her draw back, then coax her to jump by patting the top of the bar.

If she fears the bar, place the pole on the floor or the ground and WALK the dog back and forth several times, until she is no longer afraid.

During the **"Hup! Heel!"** exercise, after your dog jumps each hurdle, call out a loud "Heel!" and snap backward on the leash, then pat your side and keep your dog at heel position.

When practicing the RECALL OVER THE THREE JUMPS, kneel when you call your dog, stress the jumping command as your dog approaches each hurdle, and give praise while she is jumping.

JUMPING WHILE CARRYING

Having trained your dog to CARRY and to JUMP on command, JUMPING WHILE CARRYING should create no problem. Follow these suggestions:

While your dog is learning, keep the jumps simple.

Keep your dog on leash.

Hold the leash slack. A choking effect will cause your dog to drop what she is carrying.

Encourage your dog by stepping over the jumps with her.

Give praise while the dog is jumping.

If your dog balks at a hurdle, correct her for refusing to jump, but not while she is holding. Take away the object so she won't associate the correction with the **carrying**. Make the dog jump back and forth several times over the hurdle. Give the jumping command first, then snap the leash sharply, with praise. After which, lower the jump, give her the object to hold again, then coax her to leap over by patting the top of the jump or by tapping the floor on the opposite side.

Avoid running while teaching JUMPING WHILE CARRYING.

Keep your dog under control by making her walk at heel both before and after she jumps.

Having learned CARRYING ON COMMAND and JUMPING, your dog is now ready for the "TAKE IT!" exercise. This means reaching to take an object from the hand.

THE "TAKE IT!"

(Reaching On Command)

If your dog will reach for an object when you say "Take it!" the training outlined here will not be necessary. If the older dog has never learned to take things from your hand, or you have a dog that refuses to pick up an object because she is tired of playing games, put the dog on leash and make her sit at your LEFT side. Your dog must first reach to take things from your hand on command before she will reach to take things from the floor.

Slip the collar high behind the dog's ears, and keep it there by applying slight pressure with the LEFT hand. Hold the dumbbell, or whatever object you are using, in the RIGHT hand. When working with a small dog, squat or sit on the floor and you will be more comfortable. **Your command should include praise,** such as "Take it!— Good Girl!" Timing is of special importance. Hold the dumbbell close to the dog's muzzle and give a SINGLE command. Use a quiet tone of voice! While you are saying the "Good Girl!" tighten the collar slowly with the LEFT hand by pulling the leash UP and FORWARD. This brings the dog's head to the dumbbell. At the same time, pry open the dog's mouth with the middle finger of your RIGHT hand, slip in

 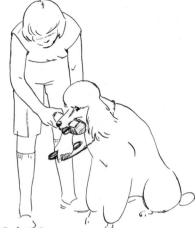

The first lesson of "Take it!" Note how the middle finger pries open the dog's mouth.

Your dog must first take the dumbbell from your hand before she will take it from the ground.

the dumbbell, release the collar, then pat the dog. After she holds the dumbbell a few moments, command "Out!" and take the dumbbell away. While working, move slowly and handle calmly. Each time you tighten the collar, increase the amount of pressure slightly, until your dog will open her mouth automatically when she sees the dumbbell coming, or when you tell her "Take it!"

The steady tightening of the collar, used for the first few lessons of the "TAKE IT!" exercise, gradually changes to short, quick snaps. Hold the leash in your LEFT hand as usual. Place the dumbbell close to the dog's muzzle, and this time, while you are saying the "Good Girl!" give the leash a sharp tug. The severity with which the leash is jerked depends upon the size of the dog, her temperament, and upon the length of time the dog has been in training for this particular exercise. If too much force is applied early in the training, the dog's attitude will be one of defiance. You will have the problem of keeping the dog's spirits up, as well as teaching her the exercise.

Place the dumbbell directly in front of the dog's muzzle and hold it steady.

Give the command in a quiet tone of voice.

Give the command ONCE.

Follow the command with praise.

While giving praise, apply slow pressure on the collar with the LEFT hand.

Alternate the steady tightening of the collar with a short snap of the leash, depending upon whichever gets results.

If your dog turns her head from the object you are holding, use your knee or your hands to block her and make her face front. Turning the head is usually the result of forcing things into the dog's mouth, instead of bringing the dog's head to the object held in the hand.

Avoid working for long periods at a time.

When you take things from your dog and she tightens her grip, cuff her nose ONCE with your free hand, take the object, then pat her.

In practice, use an assortment of articles, as well as the dumbbell.

Train your dog to take an object while she is in the down position.

Train her to take one from a standing position.

Keep in mind that **your dog must reach to take an object from your hand on command before she will reach to take it from the ground.**

When you master the "TAKE IT!" part of your dog's training, she is ready for REACHING FOR THE DUMBBELL WHILE WALKING, a grade **up** in the retrieving exercise.

REACHING FOR THE DUMBBELL WHILE WALKING

Having learned to reach for an object from a sitting, a standing and a lying-down position, REACHING FOR THE DUMBBELL WHILE WALKING will not be too difficult. Wad the leash into a ball and carry it in your LEFT hand. Hold the dumbbell in your RIGHT. WHILE WALKING, place the dumbbell close to your dog's muzzle, and give a quiet command of "Take it!" Follow with a series of short tugs on the leash with the LEFT hand, while you keep saying "Good Girl!" Continue walking until the dog takes the dumbbell, either because she reached for it, or because you slipped it in her mouth. When she is holding, come to a halt, or take the dumbbell while still in motion, and give the dog an extra pat with praise.

The instinct to chase a moving object may give your dog the necessary incentive to grab for the dumbbell, especially if you encourage her. If she does grab for it, lower the dumbbell a little each time, until she is almost taking it from the floor. If the urge to chase things is lacking, the series of tugs on the collar must be increasingly sharper, until the dog will reach on command to take things while in motion.

When working with a small dog, it is easier to practice from a kneeling or squatting position. By circling to your right, you can keep the dumbbell moving ahead of the dog with a minimum of effort. At

Reaching! A step forward in the Retrieve exercise.

the same time, the training is brought down to the eye-level of the dog.

For practice, walk backward while the dog follows, facing you. Hold the dumbbell in the RIGHT hand above the leash, which comes from under the dog's chin. As you back up, say "Take it!" then give a series of tugs on the collar with the left hand, with generous praise. If your dog reaches for the dumbbell, halt, make her sit, pat her, then take the dumbbell. If she still doesn't reach, pry open her mouth, slip the dumbbell in, halt, then pat her.

Whether working in a circle or walking forward, gradually lower the dumbbell until one end is almost touching the floor or the ground. Finally, drag one end **on** the ground.

Things To Remember When Teaching REACHING FOR THE DUMB-BELL WHILE WALKING

Keep moving the dumbbell slowly AWAY from the dog.

Give the command ONCE.

Follow the "Take it!" command with praise.

Apply pressure on the collar by tugging at the leash held in the LEFT hand.

Give praise when you tug on the leash.

If your dog clamps her jaws together and refuses to open her mouth, apply STEADY pressure by holding the collar taut. Slip the dumbbell into the dog's mouth, release the pressure, and give praise and a pat.

If response is slow, give a sharper tug on the collar.

When teaching your dog to HOLD, to CARRY, and to REACH for an object, be definite about your dog's training. When you give your dog something to hold, she should hold it until you take it away, providing it is a reasonable length of time. When you give her something to carry, she shouldn't drop it without permission. And when you tell her "Take it!" she should reach AT ONCE for what you tell her to take.

Perhaps you accomplished this training through play, and only minor corrections will be necessary. But if you failed your objective, be more demanding, so that you and your dog will make progress. After your dog learns to HOLD, to CARRY and to REACH on command, you can use RETRIEVE IN PLAY to get her to pick things up from the ground. Play combined with OBEDIENCE at this point keeps a dog happy. When dogs enjoy their work, results are more pleasing.

Encourage play retrieve but keep your dog on leash.

If there is no interest in games, owners should follow the procedure outlined in the next exercise, PICKING UP THE DUMB-BELL FROM THE GROUND. Retrieving on command is a difficult exercise for amateur trainers to teach; but if they will take one step at a time, and thoroughly master it before going on to the next, even the most stubborn dog can be taught to retrieve on command. In time, the dog will actually enjoy this exercise.

PICKING UP THE DUMBBELL FROM THE GROUND

If you have not been successful in teaching RETRIEVE IN PLAY, put your dog on leash. Sit on the ground or on the floor, and hold the leash in your LEFT hand close to the dog's collar. Take the dumbbell in your RIGHT. Play with your dog in a teasing manner. Hide the dumbbell behind your back. Scuff it between the dog's paws. Get her interested so she will lower her head. When she does, WHISPER the command "Take it!" and tug on the leash ONCE while you say the "Good Girl!" Slip the dumbbell into her mouth, then pat her.

Do this several times, then drag one end of the dumbbell along the floor, and see if she will reach for it there. If she shows no interest, tap her paws lightly with the end of the dumbbell to make her look down, snap the collar ONCE, giving praise, then slip the dumbbell into her mouth. Try baiting by rolling the dumbbell along the floor, or tossing it at the dog's feet. Place the dumbbell on a low bench or table, and encourage her to "Take it!" from there. Each time your dog picks up the dumbbell, succeeding times will be easier. Remember the **single** command and the praise WHILE THE DOG IS REACHING.

Even though your dog retrieves in play, give her this systematic training so she will always be reliable. Otherwise, whenever she doesn't feel like retrieving, she will tell you, "Pick up the dumbbell yourself!" For best results, keep the dog on leash, avoid yelling the

Bring the training down to the dog's level!

command (a playful tone is more effective), and when you tug on the leash, give praise.

When your dog will reach to take an object from your hand, either through play or through leash training, "accidentally" drop the article, and see if your dog will reach to take it from the floor. If she does, show YOUR enthusiasm by clapping your hands and complimenting the dog with excited praise. If she ignores what you dropped, kick it around and see if that will arouse her interest. If not, there is little you can do except to pick up the object and hand it to the dog with a sharper correction.

Teaching a dog to pick up the dumbbell (or other objects) is a matter of repetition and applying a bit more force each time WITH PRAISE. Take care not to become impatient, and when the dog clamps her jaws together and defies you to open them (which she will), quietly but firmly apply pressure by holding the collar taut. At this point, the dog will swallow, or open her mouth to protest, and you can quietly slip in the dumbbell and pat her.

54

Things To Remember When Teaching PICKING UP THE DUMB-BELL FROM THE GROUND

Sit on the floor or the ground with your dog and be comfortable.

Attempt the exercise first as a playful game.

Keep your dog on leash.

Give a **single** command.

Follow the command with **one** tug on the leash, slip the dumbbell into the dog's mouth, then pat her.

Each time you use the leash, snap it a **little** harder.

Whether you use the leash or whether the dog picks the dumbbell up by herself, give praise.

Try baiting! Scuff the dumbbell between your dog's paws. Draw it away in a teasing manner. Kick it with your foot.

Roll the dumbbell away from the dog. Toss it playfully at her feet.

Tap the dog's paws with one end of the dumbbell to arouse her interest.

Encourage her to take the dumbbell from the floor while she is lying down. Encourage her to "Take it!" from a low bench or table.

Train often, but not for long periods at a time.

If snapping the leash doesn't get results, try tightening the collar by using a steady pull.

When it is hot, or if your dog is excited and panting, postpone the dumbbell work until a cooler time of day, or until the dog has quieted down.

Use an assortment of articles for this exercise, not just the dumbbell.

When you have succeeded in getting your dog to pick up the dumbbell and other objects on a single command, either as the result of play or from systematic training, your dog is ready for Picking Up The Dumbbell On Command While Walking.

PICKING UP THE DUMBBELL ON COMMAND
WHILE WALKING

With your dog at heel position, hold the leash wadded into a ball in your LEFT hand. Carry the dumbbell in your right. Start walking, and toss the dumbbell to the floor or the ground a few feet ahead of your dog. Give the command "Take it! Good Girl!" walk slowly past the dumbbell **without moving your left arm, and without coming to a definite stop.** If the dog reaches for the dumbbell, keep the leash slack so you won't distract her by jerking her collar, and give extra praise while she is picking it up. If she passes the dumbbell WITH-OUT picking it up, jerk the leash BACKWARD once to check her forward movement, then repeat the command in a demanding voice. If she still doesn't reach for the dumbbell, pick it up and hand it to her; praise her, then try again.

The first command is given in a happy tone of voice, followed immediately with praise. As explained previously, praise overcomes uncertainty and encourages a dog to take things from the floor when she might otherwise refuse. More important, praise disguises corrections.

When you teach PICKING UP THE DUMBBELL ON COMMAND WHILE WALKING, it is vitally important that you do not move your left arm or lean forward with your body, until you see how your dog reacts. If she passes the dumbbell without picking it up, there is still time to jerk the leash backward as a checkrein, after which you must stop long enough to help the dog take the dumbbell.

It is equally important that praise follow every command. You will get quicker results with praise than you will with force, and your dog will respond more willingly.

For the PICKING UP THE DUMBBELL WHILE WALKING exercise, use an assortment of articles, so that picking up an object on command will not be associated only with the dumbbell. Learning to carry and to retrieve various articles also conditions your dog for the Utility Class training, which includes scent work with different articles.

Train your dog in strange locations, and don't be too quick to remove the leash. You may need it for that all-important correction. When your dog will automatically reach for a dropped object or will pick one up on a single command, whether standing or in motion, whether at home or in unfamiliar surroundings, you are ready to continue training for the RETRIEVE ON FLAT exercise.

Things To Remember When Teaching PICKING UP THE DUMB-BELL ON COMMAND WHILE WALKING

Keep the dog on leash.

When you throw the dumbbell (or other article) in front of the dog, give a happy command and follow the command with praise.

Don't stop when you come to the dumbbell. Slow up but continue to walk past it.

Don't move your left arm until you see what the dog does.

Don't lean forward!

If your dog reaches for the dumbbell, keep the leash slack, and give extra praise.

If she walks past the dumbbell, jerk BACKWARD on the leash; then stop long enough to make her take it. At the same time, use a more demanding "TAKE THAT!" and apply pressure with the collar, either by snapping the leash or by pulling it taut.

Avoid jerking the leash while your dog is reaching for the dumbbell. A jerk at the wrong time could discourage her from future attempts at PICKING UP THE DUMBBELL WHILE WALKING.

RETRIEVE ON FLAT

With your dog on leash and sitting at your left, tell her "Stay!" and **place** the dumbbell on the floor directly in front, so the dog can reach it by lowering her head. Hold the leash in both hands, low down and close to your body. **Without moving your arms,** give the retrieve command and follow the command with praise, such as "Take it—Good Girl!" The praise may encourage your dog to reach for the dumbbell, and if she does, pat and praise her! If she ignores it, the correction is one downward snap on the leash, with extra praise, after which, slip the dumbbell into her mouth, then pat her. By giving the command without moving your body, you teach your dog to **start** on the first command.

Remember, flattery will encourage a dog to do something when she might otherwise be stubborn, so be generous with your praise while teaching your dog to retrieve on command. Praise is especially important when you apply pressure to the collar.

If you still can't get your dog to pick the dumbbell off the floor on the first command, try an alternate method. Hold the leash in both hands as described above, but lengthen the leash so that the loop that leads back to the dog's collar is four or five inches from the floor. Tell your dog, "Stay!" and place the dumbbell directly in front, then give the command without moving your body. If the dog starts, give praise. If she doesn't, quickly stamp on the leash with the **left** foot to

Give the command BEFORE you step on the leash.

jerk her head down, and pick up the dumbbell and hand it to her. Timing in this exercise is of extreme importance. Give the command without body motion, and if there is no response, jerk the leash and give praise at the same time.

If your dog will pick up the dumbbell from directly in front, tell her "Stay!" and place it at arm's length. The important thing is to have the dumbbell close enough that you WON'T HAVE TO MOVE YOUR FEET when you make a correction, yet far enough away that the dog must make an effort to "go" for the dumbbell. Give the retrieve command in a normal tone of voice, and follow the command with praise. If the dog starts, fine! That is just what you want her to do. If she doesn't, snap the leash sharply toward the dumbbell, using either your hands or your left foot, and give praise when you do it. Follow by picking up the dumbbell and handing it to the dog.

When your dog will retrieve the dumbbell the length of the leash on a single command, throw it even further. Give the command, let the dog start, then run with her toward the dumbbell. When she picks it up, run backward, then encourage her to bring it to you and to sit in front. Square all crooked sits, and insist that the dog perform as perfectly as possible on the finish. Carelessness in little things creates problems later on.

By this time, your dog may think retrieving is a game. In this case, take the leash off, and hold the collar so the dog can't start until you tell her. Throw the dumbbell, and just as the dumbbell stops rolling, release her and whisper the retrieve command. The dog should dart off immediately, and if she does, don't forget the praise while she is picking it up. If she decides to chew the dumbbell, or to run around with it after she gets it, kneel, give a forceful "COME!" and follow the command with "Good Girl!" Keep demanding "Come!" and at the same time coax her by tapping the floor or the ground; but don't run after her. If necessary, turn and walk away. Then, if she comes, pat her and make her sit; take the dumbbell, and after doing so, make her go to heel position.

If your dog starts for the dumbbell on command, then comes back without it, run forward and block her. Jerk her collar once, or kick the dumbbell toward her feet, and say "TAKE THAT!" in a demanding voice. After she takes it, run backward, and encourage her to come to you and sit in front. If you think she is going to drop the dumbbell (as many dogs do), be one jump ahead of her. Tap her under the chin and say "Hold it! Hold it!" To keep your dog from getting into a bad habit, NEVER let her drop an object without scolding her.

60

Cuff her nose lightly, say "Phooey!" then take the object from the floor or the ground (or have the dog reach for it), and make her hold it again. After a few moments, command "Out!" and take the object away.

You may have succeeded in teaching your dog the RETRIEVE ON FLAT exercise in play, but to show real obedience, she must still retrieve on command while the leash is on. When the time comes that your dog will start for the dumbbell on the first command, will pick it up, and will return to sit in front without your having had to use the leash (except for a crooked sit or a sloppy finish), try her in strange surroundings. Do short retrieves at first, then gradually lengthen the distance until the dog, on the first command, will dash out thirty to forty feet to get the dumbbell.

The praise which is given WITH every command while your dog is learning is gradually delayed: (1) To the point at which the dog is picking the dumbbell off the floor; (2) to the time when she has the dumbbell in her mouth and has started back; (3) until after she has come back and is sitting in front; and (4) to the time when she has delivered the dumbbell and has gone to heel position.

Paint your dumbbell white or a bright color. On certain types of floor, or in tall grass, a natural wood dumbbell is hard to see.

Practice THROWING the dumbbell. When you release it, give it a backhanded flip. This will help it land on a wooden floor without rolling or bouncing off to the side.

Finally, make home-retrieving fairly difficult, so that your dog will be dependable when in the Obedience ring.

Things To Remember When Teaching The RETRIEVE ON FLAT

Keep your dog on leash, so you will be ready for that first important correction.

During the early lessons, place the dumbbell directly in front of the dog so that she can reach it by lowering her head.

Give the command ONCE, without body motion.

Follow the command with generous praise. The praise may even encourage your dog to start without a correction.

When a correction is necessary, give extra praise as you jerk the leash.

Give the first command in a happy tone of voice. Save the demanding tone until you need it.

When the leash is off, if your dog fails to start, reach back with your RIGHT foot and tap the dog's right flank while you are saying "Good Girl!" Then rush forward and encourage her to pick up the dumbbell.

Never let your dog come back without the dumbbell. Run forward. Block her! Repeat the command in a more demanding tone, then follow the second command with praise.

When a dog successfully learns to RETRIEVE ON FLAT, the RETRIEVE OVER HURDLE will not be difficult. The wise owner will, however, overcome as many dumbbell problems as he can before requiring his dog to combine retrieving with jumping.

RETRIEVE ON FLAT Problems—How To Overcome Them

Dog Doesn't Start On First Command

See RETRIEVE ON FLAT for ON-leash training.

For off-leash correction, give the command, and if the dog doesn't start, reach back with your RIGHT foot and tap her lightly on the right flank. Give praise as you do so, then rush forward and encourage the dog to pick up the dumbbell.

If your dog is foot-shy because you previously made a bad correction, "spank" the dog forward with your left hand, giving praise!

In extremely stubborn cases, an assistant faces the owner and her dog, and holds the leash at its full length. The dumbbell is placed between them. The owner gives the retrieve command and follows the command with praise. If the dog fails to start, the assistant pulls the dog forward, toward the dumbbell, with one snap of the leash. The owner then runs forward and encourages the dog to pick up the dumbbell.

Dog Anticipates Retrieve

Tell your dog "Stay!" and throw the dumbbell. If the dog starts before you give the command, pivot quickly and WALK AWAY from the dumbbell. As you turn, DEMAND "Heel!" The obedient dog will resist her desire to chase the dumbbell and will remain at heel position. Circle around, return to where you were originally standing, then give the retrieve command.

Alternate correction: After you throw the dumbbell, ask an assistant to pick it up and hand it to you to throw again. Or, pick it up yourself while the dog remains sitting.

RETRIEVE ON FLAT Problems—How To Overcome Them

Dog Is Slow When Going For The Dumbbell

See RETRIEVE ON FLAT for ON-leash training. When you snap the leash, do it forcefully. The dog **knows** the exercise and is merely being lazy.

When the leash is off, there is little you can do except to chase the dog, spank her rear in play, or toss something at her heels, then run forward in a playful manner and encourage her to speed up.

Dog Returns Without The Dumbbell

Hold your leash or some other small object that you can throw. When your dog starts back without the dumbbell, block her by tossing whatever you are holding directly in front of her. Rush forward, pick up the dumbbell, toss it at her feet, and repeat the command in a more demanding tone.

Dog Is Slow To Return After Retrieve

After your dog picks up the dumbbell, turn and RUN, or turn your back and clap your hands. The dog may instinctively speed up. If not, ask an assistant to stand where she will not be seen. Just as the dog slows to a walk, the assistant tosses something in back of her, then ducks out of sight. Four things are important: (1) Do not let the dog see the object when it is thrown; (2) give praise WITH the correction; (3) have the object thrown ONLY when necessary; (4) clap your hands in a playful manner after the correction.

Dog Stands Over Dumbbell Without Picking It Up, Or Stands Holding It

See RETRIEVE ON FLAT for ON-leash training.

Off-leash correction: WHEN THE DOG ISN'T LOOKING, toss some object at her feet, to take her by surprise. Run forward, repeat the command, then run backward, giving praise in a cajoling voice to encourage her to return with the dumbbell.

An assistant can make the correction by tossing the object from a hiding place, providing the dog doesn't see her do it. Having an assistant make the correction is especially effective when the dog just stands and glares at the owner.

RETRIEVE ON FLAT Problems—How To Overcome Them

Dog Refuses To Release Dumbbell

Hold one end of the dumbbell and command "Out!" Wait a moment, then cuff the dog's nose ONCE with the free hand. Say "Good Girl!" after she lets go.

Dog Grabs Dumbbell From The Owner's Hand

Carry the dumbbell in your left hand, and a small, rolled magazine in your right. When the dog grabs for the dumbbell, flip the magazine in front of your body and cuff her on the nose. After the correction, stroke her head with the dumbbell. If she grabs for it again, repeat the correction.

Dog Grabs The Dumbbell When Steward Or Judge Hands It To The Owner

Ask an assistant to hold the dumbbell in one hand, and a rolled magazine in the other, keeping both together. When the dog grabs for the dumbbell, the assistant flips the rolled magazine at the dog's nose, then backs away. Repeat this correction until the dog will quietly accept the dumbbell WITHOUT grabbing.

Dog Mouths Dumbbell

You may never completely overcome your dog's mouthing but if you follow these suggestions, she may mouth her dumbbell less:

(1) Use a dumbbell made of hard wood, such as maple. The harder the material, the better.

(2) Select a dumbbell with the centerpiece no wider than the dog's mouth.

(3) Discourage jaw movement by cuffing the dog under the chin whenever she moves the dumbbell in her mouth, and telling her "Stop that!"

(4) Train your dog to carry things that are breakable, such as raw eggs, or a small balloon. If what the dog is carrying breaks as the result of her playing with it, she may learn to carry with gentleness.

(5) When your dog is at a distance and starts rolling the dumbbell around on her teeth, warn her with "Easy! Easy!"

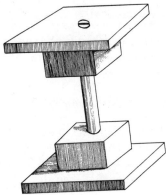

One way to teach your dog the proper way to pick up the dumbbell.

Dog Picks Up Dumbbell By The End Instead Of Centerpiece

On each end of the dumbbell, fasten a square block of wood large enough that the dog can't get her mouth around it. Tell her "Stay!" and PLACE the dumbbell some distance away. Return to your dog, tell her "Take it!" and let the dog figure out how to take the dumbbell from the floor. When she learns to use the centerpiece, gradually reduce the size of the end pieces, until you can remove them altogether.

Dog Drops Dumbbell At Handler's Feet

After your dog returns with the dumbbell, and just before she sits in front, do an about-turn and command "Heel!" Come to a halt, then command "Sit! Stay!" "Good Girl!" Practice this until your dog will hold the dumbbell while sitting at heel position. Later, when she brings the dumbbell to you and sits in front, use the "Stay!" command, followed by "Good Girl!" Eventually she won't need the voice command.

Dog Anticipates Finish After Retrieve

Take the dumbbell while your dog is sitting in front. Wait a moment, then pivot back to heel position on your LEFT foot. If the dog moves before you give her permission, DEMAND "Stay!"

In practice, take the dumbbell, then stand up straight, wait a moment, and give the dumbbell back to the dog. Straighten up, wait, then take the dumbbell a second time. If the dog starts to heel position without permission, tell her emphatically "STAY!"

RETRIEVE OVER HURDLE

Before teaching the RETRIEVE OVER HURDLE exercise, train your dog in the jumping part WITHOUT the dumbbell. Never correct for such things as not jumping, or for poor sits and finishes, while your dog is learning the retrieve part of the exercise.

Take your position in front of a low Solid Hurdle with your dog at your left side. Hold the leash in BOTH hands, as when teaching the heeling exercises. As you step toward the jump, command "Robin, Hup!" and snap the leash over the hurdle AHEAD of the dog. Slacken the leash while the dog is jumping, so you won't throw her off balance when she lands. Command "Come!" and jerk the leash toward you, with praise, to make her jump back. Run backward at the same time, gathering up the leash, so the dog will have room to sit squarely in front. If she isn't sitting straight, correct her, then stand erect. Wait a moment, then lean over and pat her. Patting your dog at this point accustoms her to the body movement she will experience when you lean over to take the dumbbell, which you will do in the regular RE-TRIEVE OVER HURDLE exercise. Stand up a second time, then command the "finish."

When your dog will jump the hurdle both going and coming, and will sit squarely in front on the return, without corrections, do the exercise while the dog holds the dumbbell. Remember to straighten all crooked sits; and after you take the dumbbell, give it back once or twice to keep the dog from anticipating the finish.

Next comes the period of chasing the dumbbell over the hurdle in play—that is, if your dog can be baited with play. Keep the dog on leash. Get her excited. In a teasing way, toss the dumbbell over a LOW hurdle and see if she will go for it. Give ONE command, and, while she is picking up the dumbbell, give lots of praise. Encourage her to jump back, and use the command "Sit! Stay!" to help her keep the dumbbell in her mouth. After she is sitting straight, pat her, take the dumbbell, and complete the exercise.

After your dog plays this game for awhile, tell her "Stay!" and throw the dumbbell. Wait this time for it to stop rolling, then see if she will start when you give the command. Play combined with obedience in this exercise gets excellent results when you have a dog with a frisky nature. Unfortunately, too many dogs have never learned how to play. For them it is straight obedience.

The next step in teaching RETRIEVE OVER HURDLE is to see that the dog not only waits for you to tell her to get the dumbbell, but also that she starts on the first command. Keep the jump LOW, and have the dog on leash. Assume your position close to the hurdle SO YOU WON'T HAVE TO MOVE YOUR FEET when you make a correction. Tell your dog "Stay!" and place the dumbbell on the opposite side of the jump, close enough that you can reach it by leaning over the hurdle. Hold the leash in both hands, and, WITHOUT MOVING YOUR ARMS, say a quiet "Take it!" "Good Girl!" If she starts, fine! That is what you want. If she remains sitting, correct as you did in the RETRIEVE ON FLAT exercise. Jerk the leash ONCE toward the jump while you are saying "Good Girl!" and after the dog jumps, lean over the hurdle, point to the dumbbell, and encourage her to pick it up.

Dogs frequently leap the hurdle when given the retrieve command, but will start back without the dumbbell. In this case, block the dog so she can't return. Cuff her nose gently with the BACK OF YOUR HAND, then jerk her collar toward the dumbbell, using a more demanding "TAKE THAT!"

When your dog will retrieve successfully over a low hurdle on leash, try it without. If she jumps and picks up the dumbbell, rush forward, pat the top board of the hurdle to encourage her to jump back, then back up quickly, giving her room to land. Straighten all crooked sits, take the dumbbell, wait to see if she anticipates the finish, then let her go to heel position on command.

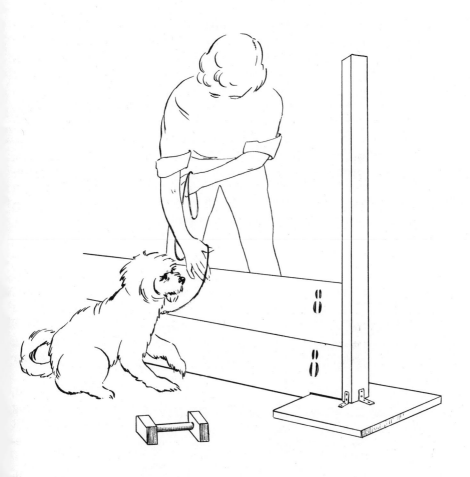

*If a dog starts back without the dumb-
bell, block her! Use the back of your hand.*

Your dog must be reliable in the RETRIEVE OVER HURDLE with the jump low, before you raise it to the required full height, which is one and one-half times the height of your dog at the withers. With certain heavy-set breeds, the required height measurement equals the shoulder height. Place a ruler across your dog's shoulder bones, and measure the distance from them to the floor; then study the Obedience rule book to see how high your breed of dog should jump.

In practice, train your dog to jump two or three inches higher than will be expected of her in Obedience Trials. This will make the required height seem child's play in comparison; but never go to extremes or ask your dog to jump unreasonable distances. A bad fall could discourage her from ever jumping again.

As you progress in the RETRIEVE OVER HURDLE EXERCISE, strive for perfection. Give one command, and if the dog doesn't start, put her back on leash and make a correction. Gradually delay the praise until your dog has returned with the dumbbell and is sitting in front. Straighten crooked sits. Even test your dog by throwing the dumbbell so that it lands off to one side of the hurdle. This will tempt her to go around, and if she does, will give you the opportunity to stop her. Only by being called back when she starts around, or by being blocked from running around the end on the return, will your dog learn to jump the hurdle both going and coming.

Things To Remember When Teaching RETRIEVE OVER HURDLE

Train your dog to jump and retrieve in play, but keep the dog on leash.

Keep the jump low for the first serious lessons.

Stand close to the hurdle so you can place (or throw) the dumbbell where you can reach it by leaning over the hurdle.

Give ONE command.

Follow the command with PRAISE.

If the dog fails to start, jerk the leash ONCE while you are giving the praise.

If the dog starts without a correction, give praise just the same.

If your dog leaps the hurdle, then starts back without the dumbbell, BLOCK her! Cuff her nose with the back of your hand, lean over the hurdle, jerk the leash once toward the dumbbell, and give a more demanding "TAKE THAT!"

Attempts to go around the hurdle on the way out can be stopped by giving the leash a backward snap.

Attempts to come around on the way back, when the leash is off, can be stopped by tossing something in front of the dog to block her. This correction should be made as the dog is passing the hurdle. If given too early, the dog will hesitate about coming back at all.

Practice throwing the dumbbell off to one side, so your dog will have to go out of her way to leap the hurdle on the return.

Practice in strange surroundings, and give the dog only a single chance. Afterward, change the location of the jump.

RETRIEVE OVER HURDLE Problems—How To Overcome Them

Dog Starts Toward The Hurdle, Then Stops And Refuses To Jump

Before you correct a dog for refusing to jump, be sure that she is capable of jumping. When a dog gives the impression of wanting to jump by teetering back and forth, but lacks the courage, suspect some form of hip trouble painful to her. Consult your veterinarian, and if necessary, request that the dog's hips be X-rayed.

If refusing the jump is a matter of being obstinate, see RETRIEVE OVER HURDLE for ON-leash training. If the leash is off, rush forward, and with your LEFT hand, "spank" the dog on the rump when she stops. Give praise as you do it.

Dog Returns Without The Dumbbell

When your dog starts back without the dumbbell, rush forward! Block her! Lean over the hurdle, cuff her nose ONCE with the back of your hand, then step over or walk around the hurdle, and, if necessary, pick up the dumbbell and toss it at her feet with a more demanding "TAKE THAT!" When she picks it up, pat the top board and coax her to jump back.

Dog Picks Up The Dumbbell But Doesn't Jump Back

Place the hurdle in such a way that an assistant can hide in back of the place where the dumbbell will land. If the dog stops at the jump on the way back, waiting for a second command, the assistant lightly tosses a rolled magazine (or similar object) at the dog's heels. The owner covers up the correction by clapping her hands in play, giving exaggerated praise to encourage the dog after the correction.

Dog Appears Afraid Of The Retrieve Command

Change commands! If you have been using "Take it!" for the retrieve, give the jumping command instead. Combine words, such as "Hup! Take it! Come!" then gradually eliminate commands until you find one of which the dog is no longer afraid.

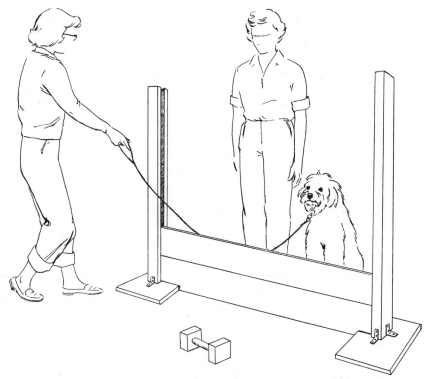

The assistant's position for the dog that won't start on command.

Dog Doesn't Start On First Command

See RETRIEVE ON FLAT Problems.

In extremely stubborn cases, an assistant stands on the opposite side of a low hurdle and holds the leash at its full length. The owner gives the retrieve command, following the command WITH PRAISE. If the dog fails to start, the assistant pulls the dog forward toward the jump, with one snap of the leash. The owner runs forward, encouraging the dog to jump and to pick up the dumbbell.

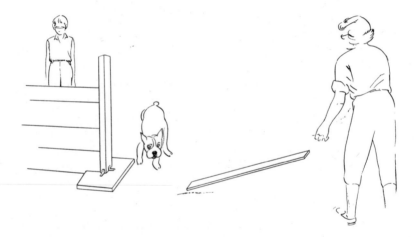

Time all corrections!

Dog Goes Around Hurdle Going Out

An assistant stands on the opposite side of the hurdle, quite some distance away, and faces the owner and her dog. If the dog attempts to go around either end, the assistant waits until the dog is on line with the hurdle, then tosses some object (a flat board is excellent) to block her. The owner recalls the dog, then rushes forward, pats the top of the hurdle, encouraging the dog to jump.

RETRIEVE OVER HURDLE Problems—How To Overcome Them

Dog Goes Around Hurdle On The Return

Make a correction first, on leash. Have your dog jump the hurdle; just as she lands, call out a loud "COME!" Follow by snapping the leash toward you to make the dog jump back. Do not make the dog retrieve the dumbbell during the correction.

For off-leash correction, the owner holds some object she can easily throw. When the dog starts to go around the jump on the return, and again when the dog's head is in line with the hurdle, the owner blocks the dog by tossing whatever she is holding directly in front of the dog. After this, she rushes forward, pats the top board, and encourages the dog to come over the top.

NOTE: When correcting a dog for running around the hurdle, it is important that the correction be made at the right time. If the object is thrown too soon, the owner PREVENTS a mistake, instead of correcting it. The dog may also be frightened, and will hesitate to come back at all.

Dog Doesn't Clear The Hurdle

If there is no indication of hip dysplasia, or the dog is not overweight, ask two assistants to stand one on each side of the hurdle. One assistant holds a light rod (bamboo or aluminum) so that it rests along the top board, slightly lower than the board itself. The second assistant is there merely to keep the dog from going around the opposite end. With the dog on leash, teach her first to clear the hurdle without retrieving. Give the jumping command, and while the dog is jumping, have the assistant raise the rod and rap her paws lightly. The severity with which the correction is made depends upon the size of the dog and on her temperament. Give praise WITH all corrections.

An alternate method is for the assistant to move a short rod from one side of the jump to the other, parallel to the floor, while the dog is jumping. This EXTENDS the jump, which raises it.

See RETRIEVE ON FLAT problems for corrections of the following: Dog Anticipates Retrieve—Dog Stands Over Dumbbell, Or Stands Holding Dumbbell—Dog Refuses To Release Dumbbell—Dog Grabs At Dumbbell In The Owner's Hand—Dog Grabs The Dumbbell From Steward Or Judge—Dog Anticipates Finish—Dog Drops Dumbbell At Handler's Feet—Dog Mouths Dumbbell—Dog Picks Up Dumbbell By The End Instead Of The Centerpiece.

THE BROAD JUMP

It is assumed that your dog is familiar with the BROAD JUMP, having learned to leap the individual hurdles in play, as described in the JUMPING exercise. To prepare your dog for the BROAD JUMP as it is done in Obedience Trials, place the individual hurdles close together and tip them on their sides. This will take away temptation, teaching your dog to clear the hurdles from the very beginning.

Put your dog on leash and leave her on a sit-stay in front of the first hurdle. Take your position to the right of the jump, with your left shoulder turned slightly away from the dog. Hold the handle of the leash in your right hand, and support the weight of the leash in your left, held at arm's length, directly above the center of the jump. WITHOUT MOVING YOUR ARMS, give the jumping command, which may be "Hup!" "Jump!" or "Over!" Follow the command with "Good Girl!" and snap the leash **forward**. While the dog is landing, command "Come! Good Girl!" snap the leash toward you, then coax her to come close and sit squarely in front. So she can do a proper finish, make a quarter turn to the right while the dog is jumping. After she is sitting in front, pat her, then complete the exercise by having her go to heel position. If your dog will start on the jumping command, don't jerk the leash, but give praise just the same. The two things to remember when teaching the BROAD JUMP are: (1) Give the command without moving your arms; and (2) give

Give the jumping command WITHOUT arm motion.

praise while the dog is jumping, whether you jerk the leash or not.

The show ring procedure for the BROAD JUMP requires the handler to stand two feet away from the jump, facing it, and within the area of the first and last hurdles. While the dog is jumping, the handler is permitted to make a forty-five-degree angle turn to the right, to enable the dog to sit squarely in front and do a proper finish. To accustom your dog to the BROAD JUMP as it is done in Obedience Trials, follow this procedure in practice as you increase the over-all length by stages with the hurdles upright, in their proper position. The required BROAD JUMP length is twice that which your dog jumps in height.

During practice, set up the BROAD JUMP in a new location. Give the dog a single chance, then move the jump again. Make her leap the jump in reverse direction, jumping from the high point to the low. Turn the individual hurdles on their backs to give the jump an unusual appearance. This prepares a dog for unexpected situations at Obedience Trials, where conditions are not always ideal.

Things To Remember When Teaching The BROAD JUMP

Keep the dog on leash until she knows how to jump.

Keep the jump narrow while making leash corrections.

Stand with your back slightly toward the dog.

Hold the leash in BOTH hands.

Give the command WITHOUT MOVING YOUR ARMS.

If the dog doesn't start, or if she attempts to amble across, jerk the leash FORWARD while you are giving the praise.

Snap the leash parallel to the ground.

Slacken the leash while the dog is landing.

At the moment of landing, call out a forceful "Come!" and snap the leash toward you, giving extra praise.

Practice in strange surroundings.

Practice with BROAD JUMPS unusual in appearance.

BROAD JUMP Problems—How To Overcome Them

Dog Anticipates Jumping Command

Alternate the Sit-stay with the Jumping command. Leave your dog sitting in front of the first hurdle. Take your position to the right of the jump. Wait a few moments, then return to heel position. Leave your dog again. Do this until the dog no longer anticipates the Jumping command. If she starts before she is told, tell her emphatically, "STAY!"

Dog Doesn't Jump On First Command Or Signal

See page 40 for on-leash training.

Off-leash correction: Ask an assistant to stand close to and directly in back of your dog. Give the Jumping command and follow the command with praise. If the dog doesn't start, ask the assistant to tap the dog gently with the toe of her shoe. Your praise and the clapping of your hands should convince the dog the correction was sort of "accidental." An alternate correction is to toss something in back of her when she doesn't start, providing she is not the scary type; but the most satisfactory method of overcoming this BROAD JUMP problem is to teach your dog that "Jump!" means jump, best accomplished through proper timing when the leash is on.

One way to teach your dog to jump higher.

Dog Doesn't Jump High Enough

Put your dog on leash. (The leash is to keep the dog from running around the ends.) Ask two assistants to stand, one on each side of the hurdle, and to hold the bar from the Bar Jump between them, directly above the jump. The height should be equal to what the dog jumps when retrieving over the hurdle. Make the dog jump back and forth several times so she will learn to jump height as well as breadth.

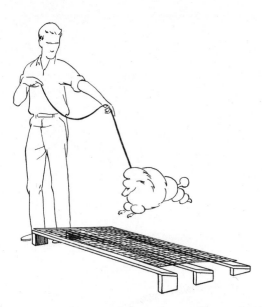

One way to teach your dog not to walk on the jump.

Dog Walks Over Broad Jump

Ask two assistants to stand, one on each side of the hurdle, and to hold the bar of the Bar Jump between them but lower than the top of the first hurdle. With your dog on leash, give the Jumping command. Follow the command with praise. If your dog starts to amble across, ask the assistants to raise the bar and move it parallel to the floor in the direction the dog is jumping. In the meantime, use the leash and pull the dog across. The moving of the bar lengthens the over-all jump and by doing this over and over, your dog may learn to leap the full Broad Jump length.

If there is no one to assist, secure a piece of chicken wire or hardware cloth. Lay this on top of the jump. If, after two or three tries, your dog clears the jump, fool her by working the wire under one hurdle at a time. Later, take it away entirely.

By using ingenuity, you may discover your own cure for the dog that walks on top of the Broad Jump. Design a jump that will "give." One that will trip. Or, place on top something other than chicken wire that your dog will want to avoid.

80

BROAD JUMP Problems—How To Overcome Them

Dog Goes Wide On The Return

With your dog on leash, and ready for the jump, give the command and the moment she lands on the opposite side, call out a loud "COME!" then snap the leash hard. After you snap it, give praise and coax her to sit close, then pat her. When you take the leash off, use a forceful command.

Dog Walks To Owner Without Jumping

Hold the bar from the Bar Jump, or the two or four inch board from the Solid Hurdle, vertically in your left hand. When the dog starts to amble toward you instead of jumping, drop the bar or the board directly in front of her. After you block her, encourage her to jump by grabbing the collar and helping her across.

An assistant can make the correction by standing a few feet away to the dog's right and holding the bar or the board in her right hand. When the dog cuts toward the owner, the object is made to fall directly in the dog's path. The owner then playfully encourages the dog to jump as she should.

Dog Cuts Corners To The Right

Stand close to the jump. Give the Jumping command and WHILE THE DOG IS LANDING, lift your knee or your foot and bump the dog as she comes down. Pat her!

Dog Cuts Corners To The Left

The same, but have an assistant do the "bumping." Off-leash corrections can be made by having two assistants, one on each side of the jump. If the dog cuts to either side, one of the assistants drops something as if by accident. The noise should make the dog veer toward the center of the jump.

One way to cure cutting corners!

SIT- AND DOWN-STAYS

When training your dog to stay while you go out of sight, leave one way, then return from another direction. The element of surprise, not knowing from which direction you MIGHT return, will help your dog to settle down and wait more contentedly.

Practice the stays as part of your dog's daily routine, and practice in strange places. Staying on command should not be associated entirely with the training yard and the Obedience ring.

Alternate the STAY exercises with the RECALL so your dog will distinguish more clearly between the "STAY!" command and that of "Come!"

SIT- And DOWN-STAY Problems—How To Overcome Them

Dog Creeps On Stays

Fasten a long line to your dog's collar. Ask an assistant to hold the end, out of sight, in back of the dog. (The line can be run through a crack in the door or through shrubbery or bushes.) When the dog inches forward, the line is jerked sharply.

SIT- And DOWN-STAY Problems—How To Overcome Them

Dog Refuses To Stay

Ask an assistant to stand behind your dog and hold the handle of the leash. Whenever she moves, the assistant jerks the dog back to position.

If the dog breaks only occasionally, tempt her so you can get in a good correction. Put your dog on a long line, and ask an assistant to hold the end out of sight in back of the dog. Tell your dog "Stay!" Face her across the training area. Kneel, tap the ground, clap your hands, run, but **don't call your dog.** If the other antics cause the dog to move, call out a forceful "STAY!" before the assistant jerks the line.

Dog Rolls Over On Back When Put Down For The Down-Stay

Put your dog on leash. Command "Down!" and pull down on the leash. When the dog settles to the floor, call out firmly, "STAY!" If she rolls over in spite of the warning, quickly lift her to a sitting position, then again tell her "Down! STAY!" When the dog will lie down properly with the leash on, remove the leash but continue with the verbal command of "STAY!" after the dog goes down, until the extra command is no longer necessary.

Dog Sniffs Other Dogs

Train your dog to stay away from other dogs! Station a dog on either side of yours, and ask two assistants to stand close to them. If your dog runs to either of the others, ask the assistant to cuff your dog's muzzle with the back of her hand, or to flick a small, rolled magazine in your dog's face. Take her back where she was and try again.

SIT- And DOWN-STAY Problems—How To Overcome Them

Dog Sits Up On The Down

An assistant stands close to the dog while she is in the Down position. If the dog lifts herself to a sitting position, the assistant quickly taps her on the nose to make her lie down again. After the correction the assistant scratches the dog's ear or pats her.

Alternate correction: Put the dog on a long line and run it through a ring on the floor or in the ground close to the dog's front paws. While an assistant holds the end, some distance away or out of sight, tempt your dog. Run, play with another dog, slam the door of your car or clap your hands. If your dog can't stand the activities, and gets up, call out "STAY!" and let the assistant pull the dog down by jerking the line.

Dog Lies Down During The SIT And STAY

If your dog lies down when you are at a distance, try sliding something along a slippery floor toward her, or toss something underneath her to make her jump up to a sitting position.

Alternate correction: Use the leash or fasten a thin line to the dog's collar, then hook it to some object above the dog's head, leaving it slack enough that the dog won't feel the pull, yet not so slack as to permit the dog to lie down.

Correct the dog that lies down without permission by sauntering back until you are directly in front of the dog; then QUICKLY reach out with your foot and tap or scuff into her paws. Follow by patting.

Lying down from a Sit, or sitting from the Down, can sometimes be cured by surprising the dog when she changes position. The owner or an assistant watches from a hidden spot, and, when the dog moves, something is dropped close by to startle the dog, making her think her movement was the cause of what happened.

NOTE: This type of correction should not be made in a training class where there are other dogs that are behaving, or they will be confused.

If your dog is not afraid of strangers, ask someone to put your dog in the correct position when she breaks. If the dog thinks the judge or the steward at a dog show will do the same, she may have more respect for YOUR stay command.

One way to overcome the DOWN-STAY problem.

One way to keep your dog from lying down on the SIT-STAY.

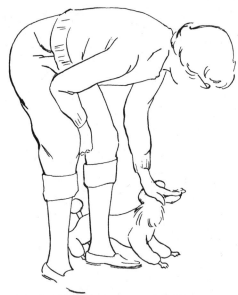

Correcting the dog that gets up without permission.

Dog Sits When Handler Returns After The Down And Stay

When you return to your dog after the Down-stay, and find her sitting, or if she gets up while you are circling, cuff her sharply on the end of the nose and put her down again. Wait a few moments, then pat her while she is in the Down position.

Dog Whines During Sit- And Down-Stays

The following suggestions may be effective, if not a cure:

1) Train your dog, as much as possible, to stay alone.
2) Use a water gun (have an assistant use one, also) and squirt water at her whenever she whines.
3) Muzzle the dog temporarily with a piece of gauze bandage. When she is quiet, take the bandage off. When she whines, put it on again.
4) Consult your veterinarian. Ask if he recommends a tranquilizer to calm your dog's nerves.

A dog that has learned to stay alone will be less inclined to whine or to break the Stays than the dog that always has companionship. Train your dog to be independent so that she will feel secure when left alone.

GENERAL Problems—How To Overcome Them

Inattentiveness

Correct your dog every time she looks away. Jerk the leash bump into her, tumble her by catching her off guard. Use any trick you can to make your dog watch you while she is in training Praise with all corrections and the dog will not resent them.

Sniffing The Ground

Every time your dog lowers her head, jerk up on the leash with out saying anything. If she is off leash, throw something or kick at the spot the dog is sniffing.

Dog Follows Handler When Left For Drop On Recall Or Stay Exercises

Carry an object in your LEFT hand. This can be a rolled magazine, or the leash wadded into a ball. When you leave your dog, ask an assistant to watch. If the dog moves, have the assistant call out "Throw it," in which case, toss the object BACKWARD, so it lands at the dog's feet. Take her back and try again.

Alternate correction: When you leave your dog, BACK AWAY. Hold something that you can throw to check the dog when she starts forward. RUN toward her at the same time, and put her back where she was.

Barks While Working

Carry a small, rolled-up magazine! When the dog barks, throw it at the dog's feet, or have an assistant toss the magazine for you. After the correction, give praise and clap your hands in a playful manner.

Dog Does Not Sit Close In Front

Use only your voice and a coaxing motion with your hands. Avoid moving your feet. As your dog slows down, or comes to a sitting position, quietly but firmly repeat, "Come, come, come!" until she moves forward of her own accord. When she does, reward her with a pat or a tasty morsel.

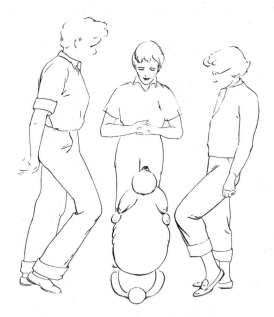

One way to correct crooked sits.

Crooked Sit In Front

Practice with the dog on leash. With the dog facing you, hold the leash in BOTH hands. Walk backward and take the dog with you. Come to a halt, wait for her to Sit at an angle, THEN pull the leash taut and spank whichever hip is out of line. The handler should CORRECT rather than PREVENT crooked Sits. In other words, let the dog start to Sit crooked **before** you make the correction. Hold the leash tight, and give praise as you do it. When the leash is off, hold the collar instead.

Alternate correction: Two assistants stand facing each other, one on either side, and close to the handler. When the dog starts to swing her rear end out of line, an assistant gently taps the dog on the hip, while the handler coaxes the dog to come close and Sit straight. A persistent "Sit straight! Sit straight!" should teach the dog to correct her own crooked Sits.

Dog Ignores Command To Go To Heel

LARGE DOGS

Without moving your hands or feet, command "Heel!" THEN with BOTH hands, jerk the leash to your left and as far back as you can reach. Praise as you do it. Pat your knee to turn the dog and make her face front.

SMALL DOGS

Lean over. Hold the leash in your LEFT hand. Without moving your hand or feet, give the command, THEN jerk the leash, low and close to the ground. Give praise WITH the correction. Pat your left leg to coax the dog to turn around.

In extremely stubborn cases, an assistant stands in back of, and off to one side of, the dog (depending on which way she goes to Heel). AFTER the owner's command, the assistant taps the dog on the hip "accidentally" with the toe of a shoe, so she will move around by herself. Both owner and assistant give praise!

Dog Does Not Do A Complete Finish

Wad the leash into a ball and hold it in your LEFT hand. Give the Heel command WITHOUT MOVING YOUR ARM. Let the dog move around to Heel position, and wait for her to Sit at an angle. THEN jerk the leash backward, giving praise.

Sloppy Finishes

For practice, hold the leash, wadded into a ball, in your left hand. Do a series of:

1) Steps to the right
2) Quarter-turn pivots to the left
3) About-turns
4) Steps to the rear

With each change of direction, command "Heel!" and snap the dog to the correct Heel position with praise.

Dog Circles Wide On The Finish When The Leash Is Off

During practice, give the command to Heel, and at the point the dog goes wide, give a SECOND Heel command, forcefully. Praise.

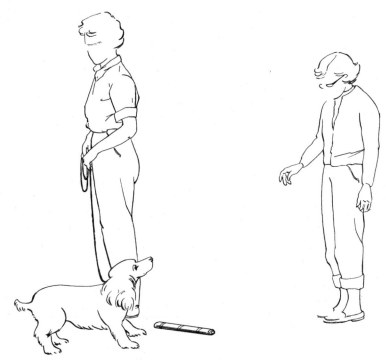

One way to correct the dog that goes to heel without sitting in front.

Dog Goes Directly To Heel Without Sitting In Front

Put your dog on leash. Face her for the Recall. Ask an assistant to stand behind you with a rolled-up magazine. Call your dog. DO NOT use the leash to make her Sit in front. Wait for her to go to Heel without Sitting. THEN have the assistant toss the magazine at your side, directly in front of the dog. After the correction, gather up the leash, make her Sit straight, then praise and pat her. Repeat the exercise but take care the assistant makes the correction ONLY if the dog goes directly to Heel without stopping in front.

The owner can make the correction herself by dropping something at her left side, if the dog is trained to go to the left; or something on the right, if the dog is trained to go to the right.

GENERAL Problems—How To Overcome Them

Dog Turns Out Instead of In, When Going To Heel Position (when going to the left)

Put the dog on leash. Give the command to go to Heel, and if th dog starts to turn the wrong way, spank her hindquarters AWAY from your body with your RIGHT hand; then pat your left leg with your LEFT hand to coax her to turn toward you and Sit close.

Dog Takes Judge's Commands

During practice, have someone call out the judge's commands Count five before you tell the dog what to do.

If you train by yourself, give the judge's commands aloud before you give the commands to the dog. This will teach your dog not to respond to the sound of the voice, but to wait for definite com mands.

Dog Runs Away

If your dog, while heeling, darts away, call her name sharply reach out and slap her across the rump, or toss something at he heels to make her look around. Pat your side! Repeat the Heeling command, using a more demanding tone and follow the command with praise.

If the dog ignores your commands and runs playfully about throw a rolled-up magazine, your shoe, the leash, anything, at he heels when she is NOT LOOKING, then drop to a kneeling position and call her to come to you for protection.

Teaching a dog to come when she is called is a family affair. At home and in the training class, cooperate by making a dog go to whoever calls her. Point to the person who called, and tell the dog "GO!" Even chase her, if necessary!

Station several assistants around the training area, armed with empty cartons. When your dog starts running around and ignores your command to "Come!" ask those who are assisting to block her by tossing the cartons directly in front of her. Kneel, call her again, and give constant praise.

GENERAL Problems—How To Overcome Them

Dog Anticipates Commands

Avoid following a set routine. For instance, alternate the Come with the Sit-stay. If your dog anticipates the "Finish," pivot back to Heel position on your LEFT foot, and don't let her complete the exercise. Throw the dumbbell, but don't let the dog go for it. Place her in front of the Broad Jump, take your position but don't let her jump. Any time she moves WITHOUT permission, DEMAND "Stay!" emphatically.

School's out!

SUGGESTIONS FOR THOSE WHO EXHIBIT IN
OPEN OBEDIENCE CLASSES

Give your dog sufficient training, so you will feel confident when you enter the Obedience ring.

Read the Obedience rule book carefully! Familiarize yourself with show ring procedure. The extra commands, signals, and body gestures you used to train your dog are not permitted in a regular trial. Careless handling can cause your dog to fail.

Train your dog in unfamiliar surroundings to prepare for the unexpected. Conditions at dog shows are not always ideal.

When you enter the show grounds, keep your dog from sniffing. If she lowers her head, jerk up on the leash to make her pay attention. Sniffing is a major problem of Obedience exhibitors.

The majority of dogs are at their best when they have been left alone prior to competing. Staying by herself even for only a few moments may alert your dog and make her anxious to please.

Exercise your dog and give her a drink of water before your turn comes to enter the ring. If the dog is to do her best work, she must be as comfortable as possible. Groom her for appearances' sake.

Take time to observe the class routine for that day. Judges usually follow the same pattern for each exhibitor. Should you fail to hear a command while your dog is working, you will have some idea of what to expect.

When in the Obedience ring, walk briskly and move in a straight
ne. Keep your corners square, and when you do an about-turn, pivot
moothly without fancy footwork. Some handlers take a step back-
ard before they turn, which leaves the dog behind.

When the judge calls for a "Fast!" change to a running pace in-
tead of just walking faster. In the "Slow!" avoid sauntering or your
og will want to sit down. When it is time for "The Figure 8" take
our position facing the judge. In doing "The Figure 8," you can go
1 whichever direction you please. Walk naturally, and let your dog
hange pace.

For the "drop," **you** be the judge of whether to use voice or a hand
ignal. If your dog faces a brightly lighted window, and would there-
ore have trouble seeing your raised arm, use a verbal command.
Vhen there is noise, and lots of distractions, give the command with
1ore than usual authority. If you prefer the signal, train your dog
o drop while your fingers are pointing up. A motion toward the floor
ould be interpreted as the signal to come; but more important, some
1dges consider an up-and-down motion a double signal and would
ail your dog, or give her a penalty.

For the RETRIEVE ON FLAT, keep your voice happy. Your dog
1ay not be reliable on the Retrieve exercise, but she **might** respond
his time because of **your** cheerful attitude.

When you come to the RETRIEVE OVER HURDLE, decide
/hether to use the Retrieve or the Jumping command. The "Take it!"
/ill sometimes cause a dog to run around a hurdle, but the "Jump!"
r "Hup!" may make her go over, and when she sees the dumbbell
n the other side, she will automatically pick it up.

For both the RETRIEVE ON FLAT and the RETRIEVE OVER
IURDLE, use a light-colored dumbbell; and when you throw it, give
backhand twist to your wrist. This will keep the dumbbell from
olling. The fact that the dumbbell is light-colored will make it easy for
our dog to see.

For the DROP ON RECALL and the Retrieve exercises, stand
way from the side of the ring, or from objects in the ring. If there is
ttle space in back of you, your dog may hesitate to go completely
round. Give her room to do a good finish.

The BROAD JUMP requires a forceful command with emphasis on the "Hup!" or "JUMP!"—not on the dog's name. Teach your dog a definite Jump command and she will be more reliable when doing the BROAD JUMP in strange surroundings.

During the SIT- and DOWN-STAY exercises, place your armband and leash far enough away that your dog won't be tempted to sniff them. If it is the LONG SIT, have your dog Sitting squarely on both hips. If it is the LONG DOWN, leave her resting comfortably on one hip. Give the Stay command and signal together, but don't use your dog's name. **Avoid yelling** and when you leave, step out on your right foot from an upright position. Crouching encourages a dog to follow.

In practice, train your dog to lie down at Heel position when you give a signal with your left hand. The left hand held close to the floor, with wrist bent, is the signal for lying down at Heel position. The dog must go down on signal or command. She cannot be put down with the hand on the collar or the dog.

After your dog's performance, if you are pleased with the way she worked, don't be ashamed to show it. If you aren't pleased, let the spectators think you are anyway! Avoid harsh corrections, or publicly shaming your dog. Obedience is a sporting game, not to be taken too seriously.

But tell me again, how do I make WILLIE take the dumbbell?